AF576794

A Garden of Choice Fruit

❧

200 Classic Jewish Quotes on Human Beings and the Environment

SHOMREI ADAMAH • שומרי אדמה • KEEPERS OF THE EARTH
WYNCOTE, PENNSYLVANIA

The mission of SHOMREI ADAMAH/KEEPERS OF THE EARTH is to inspire environmental awareness and practice among Jews by unlocking the treasure of ancient Jewish ecological wisdom.

Additional copies of this book and other SHOMREI ADAMAH publications may be ordered from: SHOMREI ADAMAH
Church Road & Greenwood Avenue
Wyncote, PA 19095

Grateful acknowledgement is made to The Jewish Publication Society and Soncino Press for permission to use copyrighted material.

ISBN 0-9632848-0-0

Original book design by Rabbi David E. Stein

Additional design by Stephen Schaffzin

Manufactured in the United States of America

Printed on recycled paper

❧

How are words of Torah like a fig tree? [As everyone knows, a fig tree's fruit ripens at various times over a long season;] whenever you search the tree, you can find figs ready to eat. So also with words of Torah: whenever you are engaged in studying them, you will find morsels of wisdom.

—attributed to Rabbi Yohanan (1700+ years ago)

❧

Contents

Preface

Few people are aware of the vast storehouse of wisdom the Jewish tradition holds concerning the environment. This volume of quotes is one of SHOMREI ADAMAH's efforts to unlock some of Judaism's ecological treasures and display them for a general audience.

This booklet is just a beginning, a taste. It reflects some of the materials SHOMREI ADAMAH has collected over the last 3 years, rather than a methodical study of Jewish sources. Most quotes are from the Hebrew Bible and from classic rabbinic writings—early collections of midrash[1] and the Talmud. That is, most of these texts are more than a thousand years old. These ancient texts lay a foundation that helps make sense of later materials—which tend to be based upon, or react to, the earlier teachings.

Nearly all of these quotes are fully referenced, pointing you to the original sources. We must be careful when removing a quote from its context to use for our own benefit. This would be similar to extracting a species from its natural habitat with no regard for the web of relationships in which it lives. Therefore, we urge you, if you are moved by a quote, to go to the text and study, to discover its full meaning.

Rabbi David E. Stein has spent hours culling our files, researching the quotes, and compiling them into a beautiful volume that you might enjoy. David is not only a master editor; he is also a master designer.

As SHOMREI ADAMAH grows, we hope to provide you with a more systematic study of Jewish ecological wisdom. For now, enjoy these choice fruits that we've picked for you!

B'Shalom,

Ellen Bernstein,
Founder and Director
SHOMREI ADAMAH

Wissahickon River
Rosh ha-Shanah 5752 (September 1991)

Introduction

As editor, I am pleased to share with you *A Garden of Choice Fruit*. In screening the texts in our files and on our shelves, we chose those deemed inspiring, relevant, and of cultural-historical interest. But I am most proud of this collection because it enables you to adapt *with integrity* classic Jewish materials to suit contemporary needs. Creative reworking of a text requires an understanding of what it probably meant when it was written down; two features of this booklet assist you in securing such an understanding: it provides you with a *more accurate translation*, and with *more of the original context,* than is generally available in English.

Features of this Collection

Translation. I have striven for renderings of the Hebrew and Aramaic that are easy to grasp. Generally I started with published translations—typically, the well-known New Jewish Version (NJV)[2] of the Hebrew Bible, and the Soncino Press translations of *Midrash Rabbah* and the Talmud of Babylonia.[3] Where needed, existing translations have been recast in gender-neutral, contemporary English. Sometimes I modified a biblical translation to highlight a special rabbinic understanding, or to express the zestful tone of Jewish spiritual texts, or to make more clear its meaning out of context. Occasionally—where a published translation was unavailable or missed the mark—I preferred to translate anew from the original text. Many insights I owe to the prior translators on whose shoulders I stood.

Source citations. To help orient the reader, locale and date have been ascribed to many sources, based mostly upon the *Encyclopaedia Judaica.* (I did not presume to list this data for biblical books.) For midrashic works, the date given is that of final compilation. The listed dates should be taken merely as a rough guide.

Accuracy. Commonly circulated translations of Jewish "nature quotes" often do *not* accurately convey the source of the original text—or its meaning. Hence every effort was made here to provide accurate translations and references. Those few I did not manage to doublecheck are marked with a plus sign (+) following the citation, as a caution.

Classification. To make this booklet "user-friendly," I have placed the quotes into groups by topic. This task required me to judge what the quote is "really about"—as if religious texts are ever about only one subject at a time! My yardstick was my belief that the quoted statements were originally meant to suggest to human beings *how to live.* That is, they are more about *people* than about *nature* per se. So a quote such as "those who are loyal to God are like trees planted by the river" would be listed under *Faith* and then cross-referenced under *Trees* and *Water*.

Layout. Each unit of thought is given its own line, to make these sometimes- challenging texts easier to grasp, and easy to read aloud to a group.

Six Clues to Interpretation

1. Hebrew or Aramaic sacred texts pack many meanings at once into terse and pithy language; each word employed can do double or triple duty as it connects together many disparate things. However, a translation can usually transmit *only one of the many meanings* of the original. So although the translations herein tell the truth, they rarely tell the whole truth; to get the whole story, you need to check the original source.

2. The context of the quote matters. What we might today call a "nature quote" was usually first uttered while addressing other topics—such as faith in God. The quote may be misunderstood if it is viewed apart from what first motivated it. Also, most of the quotes printed here are excerpted from longer statements—for example, from a sermon by an ancient rabbinic preacher. I leave it to you to look up the quote in its original context (even in translation); I have tried to give you full citations.

3. There are two general types of statements: those on *ideal behavior in a perfect world* (e.g., stories of saintly rabbis), and those on *decent behavior in an imperfect world* (such as legal rulings). Each type of statement has its proper place in life, but do not confuse them. To classify a given quote, you must look at its context.

4. Many biblical metaphors were drawn from the natural world. This helped provide a symbolic "map" for its readers to unite the cosmos—both

nature and culture, both the world of the senses and the world of the spirit, both society and God.

When the Bible tells us about sheep, birds, and trees, it also teaches its audience about themselves. Israel's place in the cosmic scheme is implied in biblical rules about animals and plants. These images lead pious readers toward a *self-understanding* that both moves them closer to God and strengthens national bonds.[4] These quotes "work" on many levels.

5. Most Jewish religious teachings are *based upon earlier texts.* To understand the import of a rabbinic quote, you must first grasp what the starting text was. If the reader will permit an informal metaphor: rabbinic culture is like racquetball; the rule is that we must bounce our mutual search for God (and godly ways) off of a wall, and the bricks of this wall are our shared, sacred texts.

Many rabbinic statements are made *explicitly* in response to earlier writings; a typical genre is the *commentary* or *gloss* (brief elaborations inserted into, or footnoted to, a text). In this booklet, I first list the prior text that serves as a "jumping-off point" and I separate it from the later teaching by these scribal symbols:

✍ ✍ ✍

Frequently, rabbinic statements are only *implicitly* a response to what has gone before; the speaker presumes that the audience shares classic Jewish texts as background. Informed audiences can discern how the new statement subtly reworks old words in order to fit a new time and place—or to expand the reader's mind.[5] In this booklet, several elements will assist you in securing the background: juxtaposition of similar quotes, cross-referencing, dating of sources, and occasional notes.

6. Religious statements can be made in a spirit of good (healing) humor; read (at least) nos. 2, 4, 166, and 168 as if they were meant to be funny.

Acknowledgements

Thank you to: Ellen Bernstein, for her determination; Toltzis Communications Inc., for its generous support; Jude Goodier-Mojher, for artwork and for the cover of the first edition; Gail Milgram Beitman, for thoughtful copyediting; Shulamit Gehlfuss, for believing that my editing religious texts required treating myself well; and my teachers and study partners, for showing me how to climb the fig tree.

Finally, a wish: may you find much wisdom as you harvest these fruits!

Rabbi David E. Stein

[1]*Midrash* is rabbinic exposition of the underlying import of a biblical text.

[2]*The Tanakh: The New JPS Translation of the Holy Scriptures According to the Masoretic Text.* Copyright 1985 by the Jewish Publication Society.

[3]*Midrash Rabbah,* transl. and ed. H. Freedman & Maurice Simon, 3rd Ed. 1983; *The Babylonian Talmud,* ed. I. Epstein, Hebrew-English Ed., 1969.

[4]For details, read Howard Eilberg-Schwartz, "Israel in the Mirror of Nature: Animal Metaphors in the Rituals and Narratives of Israelite Religion," in *The Savage in Judaism: An Anthropology of Israelite Religion and Ancient Judaism* (Bloomington: Indiana U., 1990).

[5]It is my belief that the underlying goal of religious language is to prompt us to transcend normal boundaries of time, space, and identity.

Animals

See also [18, 67, 72, 76, 82, 93, 96, 100, 101, 105, 115, 119, 156, 159, 182, 184]

---

[1] *Heaven and earth were finished—*
*all their array** (Genesis 2:1).

✍ ✍ ✍

Our Rabbis said:
Even those things that you may regard
as completely superfluous to Creation—
such as fleas, gnats, and flies—
even they too were included in Creation;
and God's purpose is carried out through everything—
even through a snake, a scorpion, a gnat, or a frog.

Midrash Genesis Rabbah §10.7
Land of Israel, c. 400 CE

*The Hebrew *tza·va* (array, hosts) connotes *rendering service* (in this case, to God), which implies that all aspects of Creation were made for a purpose.

---

[2] *To Adam, God said...*
Cursed be the ground because of you... (Genesis 3:17).

✍ ✍ ✍

"This means that it will produce accursed things for you—
such as gnats, midges, and fleas."
"Then let it produce a camel...!?"*
Replied Rabbi Isaac of Magdala:
"In that there would be benefit too—
for human beings could sell them and make a profit!"

Midrash Genesis Rabbah §20.8; §5.9
Land of Israel, c. 400 CE

*An anonymous objection to the preceding (also anonymous) opinion. i.e., if God wanted to punish Adam and Eve, why were the pests made so small—why not as big as a camel? [Julius Theodor (editor of scholarly edition)]

---

[3] *If any person...slaughters an ox or sheep or goat...*
and does not...present it as an offering to THE LORD...
that person has shed blood
and shall be cut off from among the Israelite people (Leviticus 17:3-4).

✍ ✍ ✍

Thus it is written:
The superfluity of earth with everything is... (Eccles. 5:8)
Rabbi Judah explains [these cryptic words]:
Even things you deem superfluous in this world
are also included among the things that are a benefit to the world.
For example, palm-fiber is for making rope,
and twigs are for hedging gardens....
Our Rabbis explain the verse as signifying that
even things you deem superfluous in the world—
such as flies, fleas, and gnats—
were also included in the scheme of Creation:
Heaven and earth were finished—all their array[1] (Genesis 2:1)....
Another meaning:
The Blessed Holy One in effect said to the [reluctant] Prophets[2]
"If you will not carry out My errands, I have other messengers!
With everything I carry out My errands."

Midrash Leviticus Rabbah §22.1
Land of Israel, c. 450 CE

1. The Hebrew *tza·va* (array, hosts) connotes *rendering service* (in this case, to God), which implies that all aspects of Creation were made for a purpose.
2. Moses, Jeremiah, and Jonah.

---

[4] *...If you refuse to let them go,*
then I will plague your whole country with frogs (Exodus 7:27).

✍ ✍ ✍

Thus it is written:
The superfluity of earth with everything is... (Ecclesiastes 5:8)
Our Rabbis explained these [cryptic] words as follows:
Even those creatures you deem superfluous in this world—
like flies, fleas, and gnats—
nevertheless have their allotted task in the scheme of Creation:
God saw everything that had been made, and found it very good
(Genesis 1:31).

Rabbi Acha ben Chanina explained as follows:
Even those creatures deemed by you superfluous in the world—
like serpents and scorpions—
still have their definite place in the scheme of Creation.
For God said to the [reluctant] Prophets,*
"Do you think that if you refuse to fulfill my message,
I have none else to send?
No! My message will be fulfilled even by a serpent, scorpion, or frog."
And had it not been for the frog,
how would God have punished the Egyptians?

Midrash Exodus Rabbah §10.1
Land of Israel, c. 1000 CE

*Moses, Jeremiah, and Jonah.

---

[5] *The earth opened its mouth and swallowed up…*
all Korah's people and their possessions (Numbers 16:32).

✍ ✍ ✍

Blessed be the name of the supreme Ruler of Rulers,
the Blessed Holy One,
whose world was created in wisdom and understanding!
God's wonders are unfathomable; God's greatness cannot be told!…
The purposes of the Blessed Holy One are carried out in all places
and God has not created a single thing in vain.
Sometimes God's purpose is achieved by means of a frog,
sometimes by means of a hornet,
sometimes by means of a scorpion….*
This is indeed the way of the Blessed Holy One—
to achieve a purpose by means of small things!
In the time to come the Blessed Holy One will punish the nations
by means of small things:
In that day, THE LORD will whistle
to the flies at the ends of the water channels of Egypt
and to the bees in the land of Assyria,
and they shall all come… (Isaiah 7:18-19).

Midrash Numbers Rabbah §18.22
c. 1150–1200 CE

*In the full text, stories follow that give examples with each of these animals.

---

[6] *Noah opened the window of the ark...*
and sent out the raven;
it went to and fro until the waters had dried up... (Genesis 8:6-7).

✍ ✍ ✍

Said Rabbi Simeon ben Lakish:
The raven said to Noah....
"You must hate me!
You did not pick [a scout] from species of which there are seven,
but send out a species of which there are only two.*
If the prince of heat or the prince of cold injure me,
would not the world be lacking a species?...."

Talmud of Babylonia, *Sanhedrin* 108b
c. 200–c. 600 CE

*God had commanded Noah to bring aboard 7 pairs of each "vegetarian" bird and land animal—understood to be fit for sacrificial worship—and 1 pair of the rest (Gen. 7:2).

---

[7] *Do not take the mother bird together with her young* (Deuteronomy 22:6).

✍ ✍ ✍

Scripture will not permit a destructive act
that will cause the extinction of a species
even though it has permitted the ritual slaughtering of that species.
And someone who kills mother and children in one day,
or takes them while they are free to fly away,
is considered as if having destroyed the species.

Rabbi Moses Nahmanides
Barcelona, Spain, 1194–1270 CE
Commentary on the Torah, loc. cit. (c. 1260 CE)

[8] The [intestinal] sufferings of Rabbi (Judah the Patriarch)
came to him because of a certain incident, and left in the same way.
What was the incident that led to his suffering?
Once a calf was being taken to slaughter
when it broke away,
hid its head under Rabbi's robes, and bellowed [in terror].
Rabbi said, "Go! For this is why you were created!"*
Then they said in heaven,
"Since he showed no compassion, let us bring suffering upon him."
And how did Rabbi's suffering depart?
One day a slave was sweeping the house
and was about to sweep away some young weasels.
"Leave them alone!" Rabbi said. "It is written:
God's compassion extends to all of Creation [Psalms 145:9]."
Then they said in heaven,
"Since he has shown compassion, let us be compassionate with him."

Talmud of Babylonia, *Baba Metzia* 85a
c. 200–c. 600 CE

*He related to the creature solely in terms of its "usefulness."

---

[9] Regarding anything that is needed for healing
or for any purpose whatsoever—
the prohibition of Afflicting Animals does not apply.
For example, it is permitted to pluck down-feathers from live geese;
in such a case you need not be concerned about Afflicting Animals.

Rabbi Joseph Karo
Portugal/Turkey/Safed, 1488–1575
Shulchan Arukh: Even ha-Ezer §5.14 [classic legal digest]

✍ ✍ ✍

Nevertheless, people hold back from doing it, since it is indeed cruel.*

Rabbi Moses Isserles
Cracow, Poland, d. 1572
gloss to R. Karo's legal opinion, loc. cit.

*i.e., plucking feathers is technically permitted, but it is to be avoided if possible.

[10] If you...buy new household goods or tools..., say the blessing,
"Blessed are You, LORD—our God, Ruler of the cosmos—
for giving us life, sustaining us, and enabling us to reach this moment!"
....and if it is an item you are going to wear, then say,
"Blessed are You, LORD—our God, Ruler of the cosmos—
who clothes the naked!"....

Rabbi Joseph Karo
Portugal/Turkey/Safed, 1488–1575
Shulhan Arukh: Orach Chayyim §223.3–6 [classic legal digest]

✍ ✍ ✍

One written legal opinion has it that one should not recite a blessing
on shoes or clothes made of leather—
for the animal might have been killed solely to produce this item,
and as the verse says,
God's compassion extends to all of Creation (Psalms 145:9).
Now such reasoning is weak and inconclusive;
yet many are careful not to say the blessing.*

Rabbi Moses Isserles
Cracow, Poland, d. 1572
gloss to R. Karo's legal opinion, loc. cit.

*In some editions: yet you should be careful not to say the blessing.

---

[11] The law against Afflicting Animals applies in every case,
except where an animal is slaughtered outright,
or killed for a material benefit to human beings.*

Rabbi Ezekiel Landau
Bohemia, 1713–1793
Nodah bi-Yehudah, Yoreh Déah Second Series §10

*From a legal ruling which confirmed that hunting was widely acknowledged to be cruel, yet which nevertheless permitted hunting if needed to make a living.

Cities

See also [178, 179]

---

[12] Rabbi Hezekiah, Rabbi Kohen in the name of Rav:
"It is forbidden to live in a city
in which there are no physician, no bath,
and no court that is able to administer punishment."
Said Rabbi Yose ben Rabbi Bun,
"Also it is forbidden to live in a town
in which there is no vegetable garden."
Rabbi Hezekiah, Rabbi Kohen in the name of Rav:
"A person will indeed have to give an accounting
for everything* that was seen but not eaten."
Rabbi Eleazar took this teaching to heart
and set aside funds
to purchase every kind [of produce] at least once a year.

Talmud of the Land of Israel, *Kiddushin* 4:12 (end)
c. 200–c. 400 CE

*variant reading: everything appealing.

---

[13] Rav Huna said,
"Any city where there are no green vegetables—
a sage may not dwell therein."
This implies that green vegetables are wholesome…

Talmud of Babylonia, *Eruvin* 55b
c. 200–c. 600 CE

[14] *Q:* How many inhabitants need there be in a town
to make it fit to host a small *sanhedrin* (appeals court of 23 members)?
A: 120.

Mishnah *Sanhedrin* 1:6 end
Land of Israel, c. 200 CE

✍ ✍ ✍

Moreover, it has been taught:
"A Torah scholar should not reside in a city that lacks these items:
- court of justice that is able to administer punishment
- *tzedakah* fund (to sustain the needy)…
- synagogue
- public baths
- sewage disposal…
- elementary school.

Rabbi Akiva is quoted as adding several kinds of fruit to this list,
because fruits make one's eyes bright."

Talmud of Babylonia, *Sanhedrin* 17b
c. 200–c. 600 CE

Community

See also [122, 123, 157, 167, 168, 177]

---

[15] When you reap the harvest of your land,
you shall not reap all the way to the edges of your field,
or gather the gleanings of your harvest.
You shall not pick your vineyard bare,
or gather the fallen fruit of your harvest;
you shall leave them for the poor and the stranger:
I THE LORD am your God.

Leviticus 19:9–10

---

[16] The trees set forth determined
To anoint over them a king.
They said to the olive tree:
Reign over us!
But to them the olive tree said:
Have I ceased making my oil
Whereby gods and men are honored
That I should go to sway over the trees?
The trees then said to the fig tree:
You come and reign over us!
But to them the fig tree said:
Have I ceased making my sweetstuff
My excellent fruit
That I should go to sway over the trees?
The trees then said to the vine:
You come and reign over us!
But to them the vine said:
Have I ceased making my wine
Which cheers both gods and men
That I should go to sway over the trees?
Then all the trees said to the bramble:
You come and reign over us!

But the bramble said to the trees:
If in good faith you are anointing me as king over you,[1]
come—find shelter in my shade![2]
If not, let fire break out from the bramble
and devour the cedars of Lebanon!'"[3]

Judges 9:7–15
transl. Robert G. Boling

1. NJV: *If you are acting honorably in anointing me king over you...*

2. Royal officials in the ancient Near East were said to stand "in the king's shade." In this case, the irony is that a thornbush has little shade to offer.

3. This parable is told by Jotham ben Jerubbaal, who used a common literary theme in the ancient Near East—rivalry among the trees—to publicly decry the local leaders, who had arranged for the assassination of Jotham's brothers. Further, those leaders had named a king, and the fable questions the need for a king at all.

---

[17] God hoped for justice,
But behold, injustice;
For equity,
But behold, iniquity!
Woe to those who add house to house
And join field to field,
Till there is room for none but you
To dwell in the land!

Isaiah 5:7b–8

---

[18] Like a partridge brooding over what she did not lay,*
So is one who amasses wealth by unjust means;
In the middle of one's life it will depart,
And in the end such a one will be proved a fool.

Jeremiah 17:11

*Sometimes two females of this species of bird will lay eggs in the same nest. One bird will then drive the other away, but the victor cannot keep so many eggs warm, so that eventually all the embryos die. [Judah Feliks]

[19] There are four New Years:

• The first of the month of *Nisan* is the New Year
for counting the reign of Jewish monarchs
and for fulfilling your vows to the Temple.

• The first of the month of *Elul* is the New Year
for assessing your tithe of animals[1];
Rabbi Eliezer and Rabbi Simeon say:
it's on the first of *Tishri*.

• The first of the month of *Tishri* is the New Year
for calendar years, for sabbatical years, for jubilee years,
for counting the age of your food trees,[2]
and for assessing your tithe of vegetables.

• The first of the month of *Shvat* is the New Year
for assessing your tithe of tree fruit and nuts—
per the School of Shammai;
the School of Hillel says:
it's on the fifteenth of *Shvat (Tu bi-Shvat)*.

Mishnah *Rosh ha-Shanah* 1:1
Land of Israel, c. 200 CE
transl. David E. Stein

1. Cf. Lev. 27:32, Deut. 14:22
2. Cf. Lev. 19:23

---

[20] Our Rabbis taught:
"• Those who trade in sabbatical-year produce[1]
• Those who raise sheep and goats[2]
• Those who cut down healthy[3] trees—
such people shall never see evidence of divine blessing."[4]
And the reason why?
Because people stare at them in astonishment.

Talmud of Babylonia, *Pesachim* 50b
c. 200–c. 600 CE

1. So some *Tosefta* manuscripts; Talmud reads "traders in market-stands."
2. "Sheep and goats are not raised in the Land of Israel" (Mishnah *Baba Kamma* 7:7)—apparently a land-use restriction meant to avoid soil erosion.
3. Hebrew: *to·vot* (good, healthy, beautiful; perhaps: productive).
4. Cf. *Tosefta Bikkurim*, end.

✍ ✍ ✍

[21] People are astonished at such behavior
and criticize and discredit the perpetrators—
and so public observation and protests have effect!

Rashi (Rabbi Solomon ben Isaac)
Troyes, France, 1040–1105 CE
Commentary on the Talmud of Babylonia, loc. cit.

---

[22] Rabbi Nahman once asked Rabbi Isaac to bless him
as they were saying goodbye.
Rabbi Isaac replied, "Let me give you a parable.
A person had traveled a long way in the desert
and was feeling weary, hungry, and thirsty.
Suddenly the traveler came upon a tree
covered with broad leaves that provided shade, filled with sweet fruits,
and watered by a brook that flowed nearby.
The traveler rested in the tree's shade, ate of its fruits, and drank its water.

"About to leave, the traveler turned to the tree and said,
'O tree, beautiful tree, how shall I bless you?
Shall I wish that your shade is pleasant? It is already pleasant.
Shall I say that your fruits should be sweet? They are sweet.
Shall I ask that a brook flow by you? A brook does flow by you.
Therefore, I will bless you this way: May it be God's will
that all the shoots taken from you be just like you!'

"So it is with you," Rabbi Isaac said to Rabbi Nahman.
"What can I wish you?
Shall I wish you Torah-wisdom? You have Torah-wisdom.
Sustenance?[1] You have sustenance.
Children? You have children.
Therefore I say: May it be God's will
that all whom you have a chance to influence be like you!"[2]

Talmud of Babylonia, *Ta'anit* 5b–6a
c. 200–600 CE
transl. based on Francine Klagsbrun

1. Literally: riches.
2. Literally: that all your offspring be like you.

---

[23] *If it is the anointed priest who has [unwittingly] incurred guilt,*
so that blame falls upon the people,
[sacrifices shall be offered]... (Leviticus 4:2-3).

✍ ✍ ✍

[Rabbi] Hezekiah taught:
It is said, Israel are scattered sheep (Jeremiah 50:17).
How are Israel like sheep?
Just as with a [tender] lamb, when it is hurt on the head or any limb,
all its limbs feel it,
even so it is with Israel:
if even one of them sins, all of them feel it.
Moses said, *"One person sins—*
and You will be wrathful with the whole community!" (Numbers 16:22)
Rabbi Simeon bar Yohai taught:
This may be compared to the case of men on a ship,
one of whom took a drill and began to drill under his own place.
His fellow travellers said to him, "What are you doing?!"
He said, "What's it to you? I am only drilling under my own place!"
Said they, "The water will flood us all!"

Midrash Leviticus Rabbah §4.6
Land of Israel, c. 450 CE

---

[24] *Like a pomegranate split open*
is your brow [ra·ka·tékh] *behind your veil* [tza·ma·tékh]... (Song 4:3)

✍ ✍ ✍

This is how Moses extolled the people
when they sang the Song of the Sea (Exodus 15):
"If the ignorant *[ré·ka·nim]* among you
are packed with *mitzvot* (good deeds) like a pomegranate full of seeds,
how much more so for the self-restrained *[me·tzu·ma·tim]*?"

Midrash Song of Songs Rabbah §1 on 4:3
Land of Israel, mid–500s CE

---

[25] *I went down to the nut grove...* (Song 6:11)

✍ ✍ ✍

The people of Israel is like a walnut pile.
If one walnut is removed,
each and every walnut in the pile will be shaken,
as Moses said, *"One person sins—*
and You will be wrathful with the whole community!" (Numbers 16:22)

Midrash Song of Songs Rabbah §1 on 6:11
Land of Israel, mid–500s CE

---

[26] *The righteous shall flourish like the palm tree...* (Psalms 92:13).

✍ ✍ ✍

As no part of the date palm is wasted—
its dates being eaten,
its young branches used for ritual blessing,
its fronds for covering a hut *[suk·kah],*
its fibers for ropes,
its leaves for sieves,
its planed trunks for roof rafters—
so are there none worthless in Israel:
some are versed in Bible;
others know Mishnah;
some are masters of *aggadah*;[1]
others do good deeds;
still others promote social equity;...[2]

Midrash Numbers Rabbah §3.1
c.1150–1200 CE

1. sacred storytelling and homiletic interpretation of the Bible.

2. This passage appears to be based on *Midrash Genesis Rabbah* §41.1 (Land of Israel, c. 400 CE).

Cosmos

[27] *For the leader. A psalm of David.*
The heaven declares God's presence
Of God's handiwork the sky boasts
Day after day they speak out
Night after night relate what they know
There is no utterance
There are no words
Not a sound is heard
Yet their shout rings throughout the earth
Their words, to the end of the world!

Psalms 19:2–5
transl. David E. Stein

[28] Hallelujah!…
Praise God, sun and moon,
praise God, all bright stars….!
Let them praise the name of THE LORD—
the one who commanded that they be created!
God made them endure forever,
establishing an order that shall never change.
Praise THE LORD, O you who are on earth,
all sea monsters and ocean depths,
fire and hail, snow and smoke,
storm wind that executes the divine command,
all mountains and hills,
all fruit trees and cedars,
all wild and tamed beasts,
creeping things and winged birds,
all monarchs and peoples of the earth,
all nobles of the earth and judges,
young men and women alike,
elders and youths together!

Psalms 148:1–12

---

[29] Abraham was absorbed by the vastness, the orderliness of the universe.
Studying the skies, he thought at first that the *sun* must be
the power to regulate it and to direct it all.
But evening came, and again looking at the skies,
he saw that the sun had disappeared.
Perhaps the *moon*, he then thought, was this directing force.
But again, on the morrow, he observed that the moon was no more
and that the sun had again taken its place.
Thus contemplating the cosmos, he came to the conclusion
that there must be a *Power* higher and above
all these powers visible to the eye,
who rules and guides the order of the universe.

Ma'asé Avraham Avinu [Deeds of Our Ancestor Abraham]+
(a medieval short story), pp. 27–29

---

[30] One glorious chain of love, of giving and receiving,
unites all living things.
All things exist in continuous reciprocal activity—
one for All, All for one.
None has power, or means, for itself;
each receives only in order to give, and gives in order to receive,
and finds therein the fulfillment of the purpose of its existence.
*Ha-Shem**—
"Love," say the Sages,
"love that supports and is supported in turn"—
that is the character of the Universe.

Rabbi Samson Raphael Hirsch
Germany, 1808–1888
"Third Letter" (end), *The Nineteen Letters* (1836)
transl. from the German by Rabbi Bernard Drachman/Jacob Breuer

*literally, the Name; i.e., the Tetragrammaton Y-H-W-H (personal name of God), traditionally written or spoken of in a removed, indirect fashion. In ancient sources, this name was linked with God's attribute of compassion.

Earth

See also [53, 86, 103, 106, 109, 134]

---

[31] The earth is THE LORD's and all that it holds,
the world and its inhabitants.

Psalms 24:1

---

[32] The advantage of land is paramount;
even a king is subject to the soil.

Ecclesiastes 5:8
transl. Rabbi Robert Gordis

---

[33] ...*A king is made servant* [ne·e·vad] *to the field* (Ecclesiastes 5:8).

✍ ✍ ✍

Rabbi Judah explains:
Even a king is subject to the soil—
if the earth yields *[av·dat]** the produce,
then a king can accomplish *[a·véd]** something;
if the earth does not yield *[av·dat],**
then he is of no use whatsoever.

Midrash Leviticus Rabbah §22.1
Land of Israel, c. 450 CE

*Speaking in the Aramaic vernacular, Rabbi Judah puns on the biblical Hebrew.

34] Rabbi Yose the Galilean says,
Whatever the Blessed Holy One created on earth,
God also created in human beings*....
In the world, God created *forests;* in human beings, *a head of hair.*
In the world, God created *wild beasts;* in human beings, *lice.*
In the world, God created *channels;* in human beings, *ears.*
In the world, God created *wind;* in human beings, *breath.*
In the world, God created *sun;* in human beings, *a forehead.*
In the world, God created *stagnant water;* in human beings, *sinuses.*
In the world, God created *salt water;* in human beings, *urine.*
In the world, God created *streams;* in human beings, *tears....*
In the world, God created *firmaments;* in human beings, *a tongue.*
In the world, God created *fresh water;* in human beings, *spit.*
In the world, God created *stars;* in human beings, *cheeks....*
In the world, God created *grape clusters;* in human beings, *breasts....*
In the world, God created *mountains and valleys;*
when *standing,* a human being is like a mountain,
and when *lying down,* a human being is like a valley....

Avot de-Rabbi Natan A §31.3
c. 200–700 CE
transl. Jacob Neusner (adapted)

*Cf. *Midrash Ecclesiastes Rabbah* §4 on 1:4 [c. 800 CE]— "To whatever the Blessed Holy One created in human beings, a parallel was created in the earth..."

Faith

See also [28, 97, 98, 116, 117, 131, 154, 155]

---

[35] You shall further instruct the Israelites
to bring you clear oil of beaten olives for lighting,
for kindling lamps regularly.
Aaron and his sons shall set them up in the Tent of Meeting,
outside the curtain that is over the Pact,
to burn from evening to morning before THE LORD.
It shall be a due from the Israelites for all time,
throughout the ages.

Exodus 27:20–21

---

[36] You shall set aside every year
a tenth part of all the yield of your sowing
that is brought from the field.
You shall consume the tithes—
of your new grain and wine and oil,
and the firstlings of your herds and flocks—
in the presence of your God,
in the place where God will choose to establish a Presence,
so that you may learn to revere your God forever.

Deuteronomy 14:22–23

---

[37] I found Israel [as pleasing]
As grapes in the wilderness;
Your forebears seemed to Me
Like the first fig to ripen on a fig tree.

Hosea 9:10

---

[38] The arid desert shall be glad;
the wilderness shall rejoice,
and shall blossom like a crocus.
It shall blossom abundantly,

It shall also exult and shout…
They shall behold the glory of THE LORD,
The splendor of our God.…
Waters shall burst forth in the desert,
Streams in the wilderness.
Torrid earth shall become a pool,
Parched land, fountains of water…
And a highway shall appear there,
Which shall be called Sacred Way.…
And the ransomed of THE LORD shall return,
And come with shouting to Zion…

Isaiah 35:1–10

---

[39] I will plant cedars in the wilderness
and acacias, and myrtles and oleasters;
I will set cypresses in the desert
Box trees and elms as well—
That people may see and know,
Consider and comprehend
That God's hand has done this,
That the Holy One of Israel has wrought it!

Isaiah 41:19

---

[40] Shout, O heavens, for God has acted;
Shout aloud, O depths of the earth!
Shout for joy, O mountains,
O forests with all your trees!
For God has redeemed Jacob,
and through Israel has been glorified.

Isaiah 44:23

---

[41] How welcome on the mountain
Are the footsteps of the herald
Announcing happiness,
Heralding good fortune,
Announcing victory,
Telling Zion, "Your God rules!"

Isaiah 52:7

[42] The word of THE LORD came to me:
What do you see, Jeremiah?
I replied: I see a branch of an almond tree *[sha·kéd]*.
THE LORD said to me:
You have seen right,
For I am watchful *[sho·kéd]*
to bring My word to pass.

Jeremiah 1:11–12

[43] Thus said THE LORD:
Cursed is the one who trusts in human beings,
Who considers mere flesh as true strength,
And turns thoughts away from THE LORD
Such a person is like a bush in the desert,
Which does not sense the coming of good:
It is set in the scorched places of the wilderness,
In a barren land without inhabitant.*
Blessed is one who trusts in THE LORD,
Whose trust is THE LORD alone.
Such a person is like a tree planted by waters,
Sending forth its roots by a stream:
It does not sense the coming of heat,
Its leaves are ever fresh;
It has no care in a year of drought,
It does not cease to yield fruit....
O Hope of Israel! O LORD!
All who forsake You shall be put to shame,
Those in the land who turn from You shall be doomed,
For they have forsaken the Source of Fresh Water—THE LORD.

Jeremiah 17:5–8, 13

*The Israelites live in a region with few rivers; the people are dependent on rainfall for crops to grow—and it never rains during half of the year! The presence of water is thus a powerful metaphor for life [Walter Brueggemann].

[44] Thus said THE LORD God:
Then I in turn will take and set in the ground a slip
from the lofty top of the cedar;
I will pluck a tender twig from the tip of its crown,
and I will plant it on a tall, towering mountain.

I will plant it in Israel's lofty highlands,
and it shall bring forth boughs and produce branches
and grow into a noble cedar.
Every bird of every feather shall take shelter under it,
shelter in the shade of its boughs.
Then shall all the trees of the field know that it is I THE LORD
who have abased the lofty tree and exalted the lowly tree,
who have dried up the green tree and made the withered tree bud.
I THE LORD have spoken, and I will act.*

Ezekiel 17:22–24

*This passage is the end of a much longer allegory—all of chapter 17.

---

[45] As a shepherd seeks out the flock
when some animals in the flock have gotten separated,
so I will seek out My flock,
I will rescue them from all the places
to which they were scattered on a day of cloud and gloom.
I will take them out from the peoples
and gather them from the countries,
and I will bring them to their own land,
and will pasture them on the mountains of Israel,
by the watercourses and in all the settled portions of the land.
I will feed them in good grazing land,
and the lofty hills of Israel shall be their pasture....
I Myself will graze My flock,
and I Myself will let them lie down —declares THE LORD God.

Ezekiel 34:12–15

---

[46] [In messianic times,]
all kinds of trees for food
will grow up on both banks of the stream.
Their leaves will not wither, nor their fruit fail;
they will yield new fruit every month,
because the water for them flows from the Temple.
Their fruit will serve for food
and their leaves for healing.*

Ezekiel 47:12

*This is the end of a much longer portion of Ezekiel's vision; these trees are watered by a spring flowing from a rebuilt Temple in Jerusalem.

---

[47] Fear not, O soil, rejoice and be glad;
For THE LORD has wrought great deeds!
Fear not, O beasts of the field,
For the pastures in the wilderness
Are clothed with grass!
The trees have borne their fruit;
Fig tree and vine
Have yielded their strength.
O children of Zion, be glad,
Rejoice in THE LORD your God!
For God has given you the early rain in kindness,
Now making the rain fall as formerly—
The early rain and the late—
And threshing floors shall be piled with grain,
And vats shall overflow with new wine and oil.

Joel 2:21–24

---

[48] And in that day,
the mountains shall drip with wine,
the hills shall flow with milk,
and all the watercourses of Judah shall flow with water;
A spring shall issue from the House of THE LORD
And shall water the Wadi of the Acacias…
And THE LORD shall dwell in Zion.

Joel 4:18, 21

---

[49] You plucked up a vine from Egypt;
You expelled nations and planted it.
You cleared a place for it;
it took deep root and filled the land.
The mountains were covered by its shade,
mighty cedars by its boughs.
Its branches reached the sea,
Its shoots, the river.
Why did You breach its wall
So that every passerby plucks it fruit,
wild boars gnaw at it,
and creatures of the field feed on it?

O God of hosts, turn again,
look down from heaven and see;
take note of that vine,
the stock planted by Your right hand,
the stem You have taken as Your own!

Psalms 80:9–17

---

[50] The righteous flower like a date-palm,
Thrive like a cedar in northern hills.
Planted [like the olives]* in God's Temple,
They flourish in our God's courts.
Still producing in old age,
They will be full of sap and evergreen—
Testifying that God is fair,
My rock without fault.

Psalms 92:13–16

*per Judah Feliks.

---

[51] The seas roar, LORD,
Thundering with sound
The seas are pounding with sound.
More than the sound of great waters
Great waves breaking
THE LORD is greater and higher.
Your decrees are right
Your house is an oasis of holiness
THE LORD is for all time.

Psalms 93:3–5
transl. Rabbi Levi Weiman–Kelman (adapted)

---

[52] Let the heavens rejoice and the earth exult!
Let the sea and all within it thunder,
the fields and everything in them exult!
Then shall all the forest trees shout for joy
at the presence of THE LORD, who is coming—
coming to rule the earth;
God will rule the world justly
and its peoples in faithfulness.

Psalms 96:11–13

[53] Bless THE LORD, O my soul!
O LORD, my God, You are very great;
You are clothed in glory and majesty.
God sets the rafters of the sky in the waters,
Makes the clouds a chariot,
Moves on the wings of the wind.
God makes the winds into messengers,
flames of fire into servants.
God established the earth on its foundations
so that it shall never totter.

Psalms 104:1–5

---

[54] Some go down to the sea in ships,
ply their trade in the mighty waters;
they have seen the works of THE LORD
and God's wonders in the deep.
By God's word a storm wind was raised
that made the waves surge.
Mounting up to the heaven,
plunging down to the depths,
disgorging in their misery,
they reeled and staggered like a drunken man,
all their skill to no avail.
In their adversity they cried to THE LORD,
who saved them from their troubles.
God reduced the storm to a whisper;
the waves were stilled.
They rejoiced when all was quiet,
and God brought them to the port they desired.
Let them praise THE LORD for such steadfast love,
God's wondrous deeds for all humankind.

Psalms 107:23–31

---

[55] *A song for ascents.*
I turn my eyes to the mountains; from where will my help come?
My help comes from THE LORD, maker of heaven and earth.
God will not let your foot give way;

your guardian will not slumber.
See, the guardian of Israel neither slumbers nor sleeps!
THE LORD is your guardian,
THE LORD is your protection at your right hand.
By day the sun will not strike you,
nor the moon by night.
THE LORD will guard you from all harm;
God will guard your life.
THE LORD will guard your going and coming
now and forever.

Psalms 121

---

[56] *A song of ascents.*
Those who trust in THE LORD
are like Mount Zion
that cannot be moved,
enduring forever.
Jerusalem, hills enfold it,
and THE LORD enfolds God's own people
now and forever.

Psalms 125:1–2

---

[57] *A song of ascents. . . .*
THE LORD will do great things for us
and we shall rejoice.
Restore our fortunes, O LORD,
like watercourses in the Negev desert.
They who sow in tears
shall reap with songs of joy.
Though they go along weeping,
carrying the seed-bag,
they shall come back with songs of joy,
carrying their sheaves.

Psalms 126:3–6

---

[58] Just listen to the noise of God's rumbling,
To the sound that comes out of God's mouth!
God lets it loose beneath the entire heavens—
God's lightning, to the ends of the earth.
After it, God lets out a roar;

God thunders in a majestic voice.
No one can find a trace of it by the time this voice is heard.
God thunders marvelously with this voice;
God works wonders that we cannot understand.
God commands the snow, "Fall to the ground!"
And the downpour of rain—God's mighty downpour of rain—
Is as a sign on every person's hand,
That all people may know God's doings.
Then the beast enters its lair,
And remains in its den.
The storm wind comes from its chamber,
And the cold from the constellations.
By the breath of God, ice is formed,
And the expanse of water becomes solid.
God also loads the clouds with moisture
And scatters the lightning clouds....

Elihu, in Job 37:2–11

---

[59] Rabbi Eleazar ben Azariah...used to say:
One whose wisdom exceeds one's deeds, what is this like?
Like a tree that has many branches and few roots,
so that when the wind comes, it uproots it and turns it over—
Such a person is like a bush in the desert,
Which does not sense the coming of good:
It is set in the scorched places of the wilderness,
In a barren land without inhabitant (Jeremiah 17:6).
But one whose deeds exceed one's wisdom, what is this like?
Like a tree that has few branches and many roots,
so that even if all the winds in the world come and blow at it,
they cannot move it out of its place—
Blessed is one who trusts in THE LORD,
Whose trust is THE LORD alone.
Such a person is like a tree planted by waters,
Sending forth its roots by a stream:
It does not sense the coming of heat,
Its leaves are ever fresh;
It has no care in a year of drought,
It does not cease to yield fruit.... (Jer. 17:7-8).

Mishnah *Pirké Avot* 3:17 (in prayer books: 3:22)
Land of Israel, c. 200 CE

[60] Rabbi Judah taught:
If you go out during the month of *Nisan* [April]
and see the trees budding,
you should say,
"Blessed is the One
who has left nothing necessary out of the Universe,
and who has created therein so many good creatures
such as beautiful trees,
from which human beings derive pleasure."

Talmud of Babylonia, *Berakhot* 43b
c. 200–c. 600 CE

---

[61] Rabbi Helbo asked Rabbi Samuel ben Nahman:
"I have heard you are a master expounder of the Bible,
so what does this verse mean:
You have screened Yourself off with a cloud,
That no prayer may pass through (Lamentations 3:43)?
He replied, "Prayer is like a ritual bath,
and repentance is like the ocean.
Just as a ritual bath is sometimes open and sometimes locked,
so the gates of prayer are sometimes locked and sometimes open.
But the ocean is always open,
and likewise the gates of repentance are always open.
Whenever you wish to bathe in the ocean,
you can do so.
So with repentance—
whenever you wish to repent, God will receive you."
Rabbi Anan said, "Likewise the gates of prayer are never locked..."

Midrash Lamentations Rabbah §3.9 on 3:43
Land of Israel, before 500 CE

---

[62] *Advance the tribe of Levi*
and place them in attendance upon Aaron the priest... (Leviticus 3:5-6)

✍ ✍ ✍

Thus it is written:
The righteous shall flourish like the palm tree....
They shall flourish in the courts of our God (Psalms 92:13).*
...Another meaning:
As the heart of the palm tree shoots straight up,
so is Israel's heart directed to their Heavenly Parent:
My eyes are ever toward THE LORD—
Who will loose my feet from the net (Psalms 25:15).

[63] ...Another meaning:
As the palm tree has a longing so have the righteous a longing.
What is the object of their longing? The Blessed Holy One—
At night I yearn for You with all my being... (Isaiah 26:9).
Rabbi Tanhuma said:
There was once a palm tree in Hammethan that would not bear fruit.
They grafted it and still it would bear no fruit.
A palm-gardener said to them,
"She sees yonder palm-tree and smells it and longs for it."
So they brought her a portion of it and they grafted it
and forthwith it bore fruit.
In the same way all the longing and all the hope of the righteous
are for the Blessed Holy One.

Midrash Numbers Rabbah §3.1
c.1150–1200 CE

*i.e., the tribe of Levi was promoted on account of its righteousness.

---

[64] Rabbi Joshua of Siknin expounded in the name of Rabbi Levi:
Scripture says:
And Moses could not enter the Tent of Meeting because...
the Presence of THE LORD filled the Tabernacle (Exodus 40:35).
[How can this be, if *God's presence fills the earth* (Isaiah 6:3)?]
Let me illustrate with a parable.
This is like a cave located near the seashore.
If the tide rises, the cave is filled with water, yet the sea is no less full!
In the same way, the Tent of Meeting was filled
with the splendor of the divine Presence,
yet the world was no less filled with God's glory.

Midrash Numbers Rabbah §12.4
c. 1150–1200 CE

---

[65] What is the way that will lead to the proper love and fear of God?
When you contemplate God's great, wondrous works and creatures,
and from them obtain a glimpse of divine wisdom—
incomparable and infinite—
you will straightway love God, praise God, glorify God,
and long with an exceeding longing to know God's great name—
even as David said,
Like a deer crying for water,
My soul cries for You, O God;
My soul thirsts for God, the living God (Psalms 42:2-3).
And you who ponder these matters
will recoil, frightened with the realization of being a small creature,
lowly and obscure....
And so David said,
When I behold Your heavens, the work of Your fingers,
The moon and stars that you have set in place,
What is humankind that you are mindful of it...? (Psalms 8:4-5).

Rabbi Moses Maimonides
Fostat, Egypt, 1135–1204 CE
Mishneh Torah, Book of Knowledge, Basic Torah Principles §2.2
[first comprehensive, systematic rabbinic legal code
with commentary—c. 1178 CE]
transl. Isadore Twersky (adapted)

Food

See also [12, 13, 93, 96, 128, 166]

---

[66] God said, "See, I give you every seed-bearing plant upon all the earth,
and every tree that has seed-bearing fruit;
they shall be yours for food."....
And it was so.
And God saw all that had been made,
and found it very good.

Genesis 1:29–31

---

[67] *God said, "See, I give you every seed-bearing plant upon all the earth,
and every tree that has seed-bearing fruit;
they shall be yours for food."....* (Genesis 1:29)

✍ ✍ ✍

Scripture placed domestic and wild animals on a par with humans with regard to food,
and did not permit humans to kill any creature and eat its flesh;
rather, all of them alike were to eat vegetation.
But later, from the time of Noah's children,
God permitted people and animals to eat meat.

Rashi (Rabbi Solomon ben Isaac)
Troyes, France, 1040–1105 CE
Commentary on the Torah, loc. cit.

---

[68] For THE LORD your God is bringing you into a good land,
a land with streams and springs and fountains
issuing from plain and hill;
a land of wheat and barley,
of vines, figs, and pomegranates,
a land of olive trees and date syrup;
a land where you may eat food without stint,
where you will lack nothing;
a land whose rocks are iron
and from whose hills you can mine copper.

When you have eaten your fill,
give thanks to THE LORD your God for the good land
which has been given you.

Deuteronomy 8:7–10

---

[69] And you shall eat your fill,
And praise the name of THE LORD your God...

Joel 2:26a

---

[70] Our Rabbis taught:
When THE LORD your God enlarges your territory, as has been promised,
and you say, "I shall eat some meat"—
for you have the urge to eat meat—
you may eat meat whenever you wish. (Deuteronomy 12:20)
The Torah teaches decency here:
that you should not eat meat unless you have the urge.
And you might think that you may buy it in the market and eat it,
but the text goes on to state:
you shall slaughter from your herds and your flocks...* (Deut. 12:21).

Talmud of Babylonia, *Chullin* 84a
c. 200–c. 600 CE

*Enlargement of territory is taken in a personal rather than a national sense.

✍ ✍ ✍

[71] The Torah teaches decency here:
that you should not desire to eat meat
unless you can afford to do so.

Rashi (Rabbi Solomon ben Isaac)
Troyes, France, 1040–1105 CE
Commentary on the Torah, Deut. 12:20

---

[72] Rav Judah said that Rav said:
A person is forbidden to eat
before the domesticated animals have been given food,
for Scripture says: *I will provide grass in the fields for your cattle,*
and only then it says: *and you shall eat your fill* (Deuteronomy 11:15).

Talmud of Babylonia, *Berakhot* 40a; *Gittin* 62a
c. 200–c. 600 CE

---

[73] Rebbe Ze'ev Wolf [d. 1800] of Zhitomir (in the Ukraine)
was the village innkeeper.
A Jewish wagon driver entered and asked for a glass of brandy.
As he was about to drink it without reciting a blessing,
the rebbe stopped him and said,
"Do you realize by what marvelous laws
God has produced the fruit of the soil
before it became the drink that you enjoy?"
The driver promptly recited the blessing,
and the rebbe answered, "Amen!"

Me'orot ha-Gedolim 2:26a+

---

[74] The most important discipline of Judaism involves the *blessing*.
When a blessing is recited before eating,
then the act itself becomes a spiritual undertaking.
Through the blessing,
the act of eating becomes a contemplative exercise.
Just as one can contemplate a flower or a melody,
one can contemplate the act of eating.
One opens one's mind completely
to the experience of chewing the food
and fills the awareness with the taste and texture of the food.
One then eats very slowly,
aware of every nuance of taste.

Rabbi Aryeh Kaplan+
USA
Jewish Meditation: A Practical Guide (1985)

---

[75] Rabbi Ahai ben Josiah states:
One who purchases grain in the market—
to what may such a person be likened?
To an infant whose mother died;
although taken from door to door among wetnurses,
the baby is not satisfied.
One who buys bread in the market is as good as dead and buried.
But one who eats from what one has grown
is like an infant raised at its mother's breast.

Avot de-Rabbi Natan A §30.6
c. 200–700 CE

[76] Your compassion should encompass all creatures,
not destroying or despising them,
for Wisdom on high[1] encompasses all created things—
minerals, plants, animals, and human beings!
This is the reason behind the Rabbis warning us
about lack of respect for our sources of food.[2]
Because Wisdom on high disrespects nothing—
everything being derived from there, as it is written,
You have made them all via Wisdom (Psalms 104:24)[3]—
it is fitting that our compassion should also take in all God's works[4]
....Thus, you should not uproot anything that grows
nor kill any living thing unless it is needed [for food].
And you should choose a quick and easy death for them,
with a knife carefully inspected,[5]
to have compassion on them as far as possible.
To sum up: The principle of Wisdom
is that love should be extended to everything that exists,
so that you do not harm them but rather elevate them ever higher,
from plant to animal and from animal to human.[6]
For only then it is permitted to uproot the plant and to kill the beast,
to transform a loss into a gain.

Rabbi Moses Cordovero
Safed, Land of Israel, 1522–1570
Tomér Devorah [Deborah's Palm Tree] §3 (end)
[an ethical tract based on mysticism]
transl. based on Rabbi Louis Jacobs, with assistance from Miles Krassen

1. In *kabbalah* (Jewish mysticism): the primal point of emanation for God's creating and sustaining power; the second *sefirah* (stage or aspect of divine being).

2. Talmud of Babylonia, *Berakhot* 50b.

3. NJV: *You have made them all with wisdom.*

4. i.e., the proper state of awareness with regard to food is one wherein all of Creation is included in an undifferentiated way, so that you feel lovingly connected to all things, including what you are preparing to eat.

5. Animals are to be slaughtered per classic rabbinic regulations, where the knife must be free of nicks that might tear at the flesh and increase pain.

6. Each step in the food chain is also a spiritual elevation; you elevate what you eat because it becomes part of you.

Land of Israel

See also [68, 46, 48]

---

[77] And Abram took his wife Sarai...
and all the wealth they had amassed...
and they set out for the land of Canaan...
And Abram passed through the land
as far as the site of Shechem,
at the terebinth of Moreh.*

Genesis 12:5–6

*Or: terebinth of teaching.

---

[78] The famine in the land was severe.
And when they had eaten up the rations
that they had brought from Egypt,
their father [Israel] said to them,
"Go again and procure some food for us....
Take some of the choice products of the land in your baggage,
and carry them down [to Egypt] as a gift for the man—
some balm and some honey, gum, ladanum,
pistachio nuts, and almonds...

Genesis 43:11

---

[79] A time is coming —declares God—
When the plowhand shall meet the reaper,*
And the treader of grapes
The one who holds the [bag of] seed;
When the mountains shall drip wine
And all the hills shall wave [with grain].

I will restore My people Israel…
I will plant them upon their soil,
Nevermore to be uprooted
From the soil I have given them —said your God.

Amos 9:13–15

*i.e., the crops will be so bountiful that the harvest will not yet be completed when it comes time to plant again.

---

[80] Prophecy about the Land of Israel,
and say to the mountains and the hills,
to the watercourses and to the valleys,
"Thus said THE LORD God:….
'You, O Mountains of Israel,
shall yield your produce
and bear your fruit for My people Israel,
for their return is near.
For I will care for you:
I will turn to you,
and you shall be tilled and sown.
I will settle a large population on you,
the whole House of Israel;
the towns shall be resettled, and the ruined sites rebuilt….
And you shall know that I am THE LORD.'"

Ezekiel 36:6–11

---

[81] Thus said THE LORD God:
Moreover, in this I will respond to the House of Israel
and act for their sake:
I will multiply their people like sheep.
As Jerusalem is filled with sacrificial sheep during her festivals,
so shall the ruined cities be filled with flocks of people.
And they shall know that I am THE LORD.

Ezekiel 36:37–38

[82] *The land that you are about to invade and occupy*
is not like the land of Egypt from which you have come (Deut. 11:10).

✍ ✍ ✍

....Now Scripture says,
I *gave you a desirable land—*
the fairest heritage [na·cha·lat tzvi] *of all the nations...* (Jeremiah 3:19)
As the deer *[tzvi]* is swifter than any other animal—domestic or wild—
so the produce of the Land of Israel grows more swiftly
than that of any other land.
Another meaning: Just as the hide of the deer,
once separated from the flesh, cannot contain it,[1]
so also the Land of Israel cannot contain all its produce
so long as Israel is occupied with Torah.[2,3]
Just as deer meat is the easiest to digest of all animals—domestic or wild—
so the produce of the Land of Israel is easier to digest
than that of any other land.
You might think that since it is easy to digest, it is not rich;
hence Scripture says, *A land flowing with milk and honey* (Deut. 11:9)—
rich as milk and sweet as honey....

Midrash Sifré to Deuteronomy §37 *(Ekev)*
Land of Israel, c. 400 CE

1. The hide shrinks.

2. *If you follow My laws...the earth shall yield its produce and the trees of the field their fruit....[Harvests will be so bountiful that] you shall have to clear out the old to make room for the new* (Lev. 26:3-4, 10).

3. Cf. Talmud of Babylonia, *Ketubbot* 112a (Rav Hisda).

---

[83] Rabbi Hiyya ben Ashi stated in the name of Rav:
In the future, all the barren[1] trees in the Land of Israel will bear fruits—
as it is said,
...The trees have borne their fruit;
Fig tree and vine have yielded their strength (Joel 2:22).[2]

Talmud of Babylonia, *Ketubbot* 112b (end)
c. 200–c. 600 CE

1. any species that does not bear edible fruit or nuts.

2. The verse is interpreted as if its two parts were mutually exclusive; since food trees are mentioned in the second part, then the first part must refer to barren trees.

Mountains

See also [41, 55, 56, 80, 132]

---

[84] The voice of THE LORD is over the waters;
the God of glory thunders,
THE LORD, over the mighty waters.
The voice of THE LORD...breaks cedars;
THE LORD shatters the cedars of Lebanon—
making Lebanon skip like a calf,
Sirion, like a young wild ox.
The voice of THE LORD...convulses the wilderness;
THE LORD convulses the wilderness of Kadesh;
the voice of THE LORD causes hinds to calve,
brings ewes to early birth;*
while in the Temple all say, "Glory!"

Psalms 29:3–9

*or: and strips forests bare.

Place of Humans

See also [2, 3, 10, 11, 31, 32, 33, 34, 65, 113, 200]

---

[85] ...*no tree* [si·ach][1] *of the field being yet on the earth...* (Genesis 2:5)

✍ ✍ ✍

All trees converse *[me·si·chim]* (so to speak) with one another;
all trees converse (so to speak) with humankind.
All trees were created for human companionship[2]....

Midrash Genesis Rabbah §13.2
Land of Israel, c. 400 CE

1. An unusual word for "tree," which is what prompts the following comments.
2. Other manuscripts: human enjoyment. Still others: human hurt.
[See notes by Theodor/Albeck and Mirkin in their scholarly editions]

---

[86] ... *THE LORD God had not sent rain upon the earth,*
and there were no people to till the soil... (Genesis 2:5).

✍ ✍ ✍

Rabbi Simeon bar Yohai said:
Three things are equal in importance:
earth, humans, and rain.
Rabbi Levi ben Hiyyata said:
And these three each consist of three letters [in Hebrew],
to teach that without earth, there is no rain
and without rain, earth cannot endure;
while without either, humans cannot exist.

Midrash Genesis Rabbah §13.3
Land of Israel, c. 400 CE

---

[87] Then THE LORD God formed a human *[a·dam]*
from clods of humus *[a·da·mah]*
and blew into the nostrils the breath of life.
Thus the human became a living being.

Genesis 2:7

---

[88] *...and the tree of knowledge of good and bad* (Genesis 2:9).

✍ ✍ ✍

What was the tree from which Adam and Eve ate?
Rabbi Meir said, "It was wheat...."
Rabbi Judah ben Rabbi Ila'i said, "They were grapes...."
Rabbi Abba of Acco said, "It was the citron...."
Rabbi Jose said, "They were figs...."
Rabbi Azariah and Rabbi Judah ben Rabbi Simon
in the name of Rabbi Joshua ben Levi said,
"Heaven forbid that we should deduce what the tree was!
The Blessed Holy One did not, and will not, reveal what it was."*

Midrash Genesis Rabbah §15.7
Land of Israel, c. 400 CE

*So that it might not be said, "Through this tree death came into the world."

---

[89] THE LORD God took and placed the human being
in the garden of Eden,
to till it and tend it.*

Genesis 2:15

*Or: to work it and watch over it [Rabbi Gershon Winkler].

---

[90] When the woman saw that the tree was good for eating
and a delight to eyes,
and that the tree was desirable as a source of wisdom,
she took of its fruit and ate.
She also gave some to her husband, and he ate.
Then the eyes of both of them were opened
and they perceived that they were naked;
and they sewed together fig leaves
and made themselves loincloths.

Genesis 3:6–7

---

[91] And THE LORD God said,
"Now that the human beings have become like any of us,
knowing good and bad,
what if they should stretch out their hand
and take also from the tree of life and eat, and live forever!"
So THE LORD God banished them from the garden of Eden,

to till the soil from which they were taken.
God drove the human beings out,
and stationed east of the garden of Eden
the cherubim* and the fiery ever-turning sword,
to guard the way to the tree of life.

Genesis 3:6–33

*Winged beings that in the ancient Near East were understood to protect sacred places.

---

[92] Noah built an altar to THE LORD and—
taking of every clean animal and of every clean bird—
he offered burnt offering on the altar.
THE LORD smelled the pleasing odor,
and THE LORD made an inward promise:
"Never again will I doom the earth because of human beings,
since the devisings of the human mind are evil from youth;
nor will I ever again destroy every living being, as I have done.
So long as the earth endures,
Seedtime and harvest,
Cold and heat,
Summer and winter,
Day and night
Shall not cease."

Genesis 8:20–22

---

[93] God blessed Noah and his children, and said to them,
"Be fertile and increase, and fill the earth.
The fear and the dread of you
shall be upon all the beasts of the earth
and upon all the birds of the sky—
everything with which the earth is astir—
and upon all the fish of the sea;
they are given into your hand.
Every creature that lives shall be yours to eat;
as with the green grasses, I give you all these.
You must not, however, eat flesh with its life-blood in it.
And for your own life-blood I will require a reckoning:
I will require it of every beast.
Of human beings too I will require a reckoning for human life…"

Genesis 9:1–5

[94] The land must not be sold beyond reclaim,
for the land is Mine;
you are but strangers resident with Me.
Throughout the land that you hold,
you must provide for its redemption.

Leviticus 25:23–4

---

[95] Thus said THE LORD,
the Creator of heaven who alone is God,
Who formed the earth and made it,
Who alone established it—
Who did not create it a waste,
but formed it for habitation…

Isaiah 45:18

---

[96] You make springs gush forth in torrents;
They make their way between the hills
Giving drink to all the wild beasts;
The wild asses slake their thirst.
The birds of the sky dwell beside them
And sing among the foliage.…
You make the grass grow for the cattle
and herbage for human labor
that people may get food from the earth
wine that cheers the human heart
oil that makes the face shine
and bread that sustains human life.
The trees of THE LORD drink their fill,
the cedars of Lebanon, God's own planting,
where birds make their nests;
the stork has her home in the junipers.
The high mountains are for wild goats;
the crags are a refuge for rock-badgers.

Psalms 104:10–18

---

[97] How many are the things You have made, O LORD!
You have made them all with wisdom;
the earth is full of Your creations.
There is the sea, vast and wide,

with its creatures beyond number,
living things, small and great.
There go the ships,
and whales* that You formed to sport with.

Psalms 104:24–26

*NJV: Leviathan.

---

[98] All creatures look to You
To give them their food when it is due....
Take away their breath, they perish
and turn again to dust;
Send back Your breath, they are created,
and You renew the face of the earth....
I will sing to THE LORD as long as I live;
all my life I will chant hymns to my God!

Psalms 104:27–30

---

[99] THE LORD replied to Job out of the tempest and said:....
Who closed the sea behind doors
When it gushed forth out of the womb,
When I clothed it in clouds,
Swaddled it in dense clouds,
When I made breakers My limit for it,
And set up its bars and doors,
And said, "You may come so far and no farther;
Here your surging waves will stop"?....
Does the rain have a father?
Who begot the dewdrops?
From whose belly came forth the ice?
Who gave birth to the frost of heaven?....
Who is wise enough to give an account of the heavens?
Who can tilt the bottles of the sky—
Whereupon the earth melts into a mass,
And its clods stick together?

Job 38:1, 8–11, 28–30, 37–38

---

[100] THE LORD replied to Job out of the tempest and said:....
Who provides food for the raven
When its young cry out to God
And wander about in search of food?

Do you know the season when the mountain goats give birth?
Can you mark the time when the hinds calve?....
Their young are healthy; they grow up in the open;
They leave and return no more.
Who sets the wild ass free?
Who loosens the bonds of the onager?....
They roam the hills for their pasture;
searching for any green thing....
The wing of the ostrich beats joyously;
Are her pinions and plumage like the stork's?....
Do you give the horse his strength?
Do you clothe his neck with a mane?....
Does the eagle soar at your command,
Building its nest high,
Dwelling in the rock...?
....Job said in reply to THE LORD:
See, I am of small worth; what can I answer you?

Job 38:1, 41; 39:1, 4–5, 8, 13, 19, 27–28, 40:3–4

---

[101] Why were human beings created last [in the order of Creation]?....
....Another meaning:
So they should not grow proud—
for one can say to them,
"The gnat came before you in the Creation!"
Another meaning:
So they might immediately begin fulfilling a *mitzvah*.*
Another meaning:
So they might enter the [already prepared] banquet at once.
An analogy: What is this like?
Like a ruler who built a palace, dedicated it, prepared a meal,
and only then invited the guests....

Tosefta Sanhedrin 8:4–5 [ed. Lieberman 8:8–9]
Land of Israel, c. 400 CE
Similarly in Talmud of Babylonia, *Sanhedrin* 38a

**Mitzvah:* what God requires of Jews: in this case, keeping the Sabbath holy.

---

[102] *My beloved has gone down to his garden,*
To the beds of spices,
To browse in the gardens
And to pick lilies (Song 6:2).

✍ ✍ ✍

Rabbi Yose ben Rabbi Hanina said....
My beloved refers to the Blessed Holy One;
to his garden refers to the world;
to the beds of spices means Israel;
to browse in the gardens means synagogues and houses of study;
and to pick lilies—to take away the righteous in Israel.
What is the difference between the death of the old and of the young?....
Rabbi Abbahu said:
If a fig is picked when ripe, it is good for itself and good for the tree.
But if picked while still unripe, it is bad for itself and bad for the tree.

Midrash Song of Songs Rabbah §1 on 6:2
Land of Israel, mid–500s CE

---

[103] Rabbi Eleazar said:
"A human who owns no land is no human;
as the Bible says,
The heavens are THE LORD's heavens,
while the earth was given to human beings (Psalms 115:16)..."

Talmud of Babylonia, *Yebamot* 63a
c. 200–c. 600 CE

---

[104] Rav Hisda and Rabbah bar Rav Huna sat all day long
as judges in court, and their hearts grew faint.
Rav Hiyya bar Rav of Difti recited to them:
Moses sat as magistrate among the people,
while they stood about Moses from morning until evening (Ex. 18:13).
Now do you really think that Moses sat in judgment all day long—
when then would he have had time to study his Torah?
What the text means to tell us is this:
Every judge who judges with complete fairness for even a single hour
is counted by Scripture as if having been made
a partner in Creation with the Blessed Holy One:
[The Torah draws the parallel via this similarity of phrasing—]
here in Exodus 18:13 it is written,
from morning until evening (min ha-bo·ker ad ha-e·rev)
and in Genesis 1:5 it is written,
there was evening and there was morning
(vay·hi e·rev vay·hi vo·ker)—*a first day.*

Talmud of Babylonia, *Shabbat* 10a
c. 200–c. 600 CE

[105] Six sounds carry from one end of the world to the other,
yet this sound cannot be heard:[1,2]
• When people cut down the trunk of a tree that yields food,
the sound goes out from one end of the world to the other,
yet this sound cannot be heard;
• When a snake sheds its skin...
• When a woman is divorced from her husband[3]...
• When a wife has sex with her husband for the first time...
• When an infant comes out of its mother's womb...
• When the soul departs from the body, the sound goes out from one end of the world to the other, yet this sound cannot be heard.
The soul does not leave the body until it beholds the divine Presence—
...*a person may not see Me and live* (Exodus 33:20).

Pirké de-Rabbi Eliezer §34
Land of Israel, c. 700–750 CE

1. Cf. Psalms 19:4-5—*Not a sound is heard/Yet their shout rings throughout the earth/Their words, to the end of the world.*

2. These items seem to relate loosely to Adam & Eve [Shulamit Gehlfuss]. Cf. *Midrash Genesis Rabbah* §6.7 (lists 3 items); Talmud of Babylonia, *Yoma* 20b (lists 4 items).

3. Cf. Malachi 2:14-16.

---

[106] *One generation goes, another comes,*
but the earth abides forever (Ecclesiastes 1:4).

✍ ✍ ✍

Rabbi Judah ben Korchah said:
One could argue that the verse should have read,
"The *earth* goes and the *earth* comes,
and the *generation* abides forever"—
because which was created for the sake of which?
The *earth* was created for the sake of a *generation*!*
But a *generation* doesn't abide by God's commands—
hence it decays;
whereas the *earth* abides by God's commands—
hence it does not decay.

Midrash Ecclesiastes Rabbah §4 on 1:4
c. 800 CE

*i.e., for the sake of human beings.

[107] The world is a tree, and human beings are its fruit.

Rabbi Solomon ibn Gabirol+
Malaga, Spain, c. 1020–c. 1057

---

[108] Inwardly, the proud person says:
"I am a writer, I am a singer, I am a great one at studying."
Since such people will not turn to God—
not even on the threshold of hell—
they are reborn again as bees,
which hum and buzz:
"I am, I am, I am."

Rebbe Raphael of Bershad+
Podolia, Ukraine, d. c. 1821

---

[109] Two people were once fighting over a piece of land.
Each claimed ownership,
and each bolstered the claim with apparent proof.
After arguing for a long time,
they agreed to resolve their conflict by putting the case before a rabbi.
The rabbi sat as an arbitrator and listened carefully,
but despite years of legal training
the rabbi could not reach a decision.
Both parties seemed to be right.
Finally the rabbi said,
"Since I cannot decide to whom this land belongs, let's ask the land."
The rabbi put an ear to the ground, and after a moment stood up.
"My friends, the land says it belongs to neither of you—
but that *you* belong to *it*."

Source unknown

Plants

See also [38, 66, 67, 76, 78, 93, 126, 135, 136, 158, 159, 160, 170, 171, 172]

---

[110] Come, my beloved,
Let us go into the open;
Let us lodge among the henna shrubs.
Let us go early to the vineyards;
Let us see if the vine has flowered,
If its blossoms have opened,
If the pomegranates are in bloom...

Song of Songs 7:12–13

---

[111] Every blade of grass sings poetry to God
without ulterior motives or alien thoughts—
without consideration of reward.
How good and lovely it is, then,
when one is able to hear this song of the grasses.
It is therefore a precious thing
to conduct oneself with piety
when strolling among them.

Rebbe Nahman of Bratslav+
Podolia, Ukraine, 1772–1810
Likkutei MoHaRaN: Rabbi Nahman's Wisdom, p. 306

---

[112] It is especially precious
to go out into the fields at the beginning of spring,
when nature awakens from her sleep,
and to pour out a prayer there.
For every fresh blade of grass, every new flower,
all join themselves with the prayer,
for they too yearn and long for God.

Rebbe Nahman of Bratslav+
Podolia, Ukraine, 1772–1810
Maggid Sichot, p. 48

Rain

See also [47, 58, 86, 99]

---

[113] On account of three things does rain fall:

- for the sake of the land
- for the sake of God's lovingkindness
- for the sake of God's corrective trials.

All three are mentioned in these verses:
God...loads the clouds with moisture....
And scatters lightning clouds
Causing each of them to happen to God's land,
whether as a scourge or as a blessing (Job 37:11, 13).

Talmud of the Land of Israel, *Ta'anit* 3:3
c. 200–c. 400 CE

---

[114] ...*THE LORD God had not sent rain upon the earth,*
and there were no people to till the soil... (Genesis 2:5).

✍ ✍ ✍

....A certain Gentile asked Rabbi Joshua:
"You have festivals and we have festivals;
we do not rejoice when you do, and you do not rejoice when we do—
when do we both rejoice together?"
"When the rain falls."
And what is the proof?
You soften the earth with showers,
You bless its growth....
The meadows are clothed with flocks,
the valleys mantled with grain;
they raise a shout, they break into song (Psalms 65:11-14).
And what follows?
Raise a shout for God, all the earth! (Psalms 66:1)—
not *priests, Levites,* or *Israelites* is written here, but *all the earth.*

Midrash Genesis Rabbah §13.6
Land of Israel, c. 400 CE

[115] *Praise THE LORD, all you nations;*
extol God, all you peoples;
for great is God's steadfast love toward us;
the faithfulness of THE LORD endures forever!
Hallelujah! (Psalms 117)

✍ ✍ ✍

Rabbi Tanhum ben Chiyya taught:
The sending of rain is an event
greater than the giving of the Torah.
The Torah was a joy for Israel only,
but rain gives joy to the entire world,
including animals and birds—
as it is said:
You take care of the earth and irrigate it… (Psalms 65:10).

Midrash Psalms 117
Italy, c. 900–c. 1300 CE

Security

See also [79, 138, 169]

---

[116] In that day,
I will make a covenant for them[1]
with the beasts of the field, the birds of the air,
and the creeping things of the ground;
I will also banish bow, sword, and war from the land.
Thus I will let them lie down in safety.

And I will espouse you forever:
I will espouse you with righteousness and justice,
And with goodness and mercy,
And I will espouse you with faithfulness;[2]
Then you shall be devoted to THE LORD.

Hosea 2:20–22

1. namely, the people of the northern kingdom of Israel.
2. God (the groom) will give these qualities to Israel (the bride) as the bride price.

---

[117] I will heal their affliction,
Generously will I take them back in love;
For My anger has turned away from them.
I will be to Israel like dew;
They shall blossom like the lily,
striking root like a Lebanon tree.
Their boughs shall spread out far,
Their beauty shall be like the olive tree's,
and fragrance like that of Lebanon.
Those who sit in their shade shall be revived:
They shall bring to life new grain,
They shall blossom like the vine;
Their scent shall be like the wine of Lebanon.

Hosea 14:5–8

[118] All the days of Solomon,
Judah and Israel from Dan to Beer-Sheba dwelt in safety,
everyone under their own vine and under their own fig tree.

I Kings 5:5

---

[119] They shall build houses and dwell in them,
They shall plant vineyards and enjoy their fruit...
For the days of my people shall be
as long as the days of a tree,
My chosen ones shall outlive
the work of their hands....
The wolf and the lamb shall graze together,
And the lion shall eat straw like the ox,
And the serpent's food shall be earth.
In all my sacred mount
Nothing evil or vile shall be done —said God.

Isaiah 65:21–25

Special Times

See also [19, 60, 134, 159]

---

[120] Mark, on the fifteenth day of the seventh month,
when you have gathered in the yield of your land,
you shall observe the festival of THE LORD for seven days:
a complete rest on the first day,
and a complete rest on the eighth day.
On the first day you shall take the product of *hadar* trees,[1]
branches of palm trees,
boughs of leafy trees,
and willows of the brook,
and you shall rejoice before THE LORD your God seven days....
You shall live in booths *[sukkot]* seven days;
all citizens in Israel shall live in booths,
in order that future generations may know
that I made the Israelite people live in booths
when I brought them out of the land of Egypt,[2]
I THE LORD your God.

Leviticus 23:39–43

1. Traditionally understood to be the citron.

2. At this time of year, 20th-century nomadic shepherds in the Sinai move from the wilderness to oases, for it is the end of the dry season and water is not found elsewhere. There, the nomads leave their tents and set up camp in booths. Built of palm wood and palm fronds, the booths are more durable and convenient than tents. Presumably this was also the practice of the ancient Israelites. [Nogah Hareuveni]

---

[121] When you enter the land that I give you,
The land shall observe a sabbath of THE LORD.
Six years you may sow your field
and six years you may prune your vineyard
and gather in the yield.
But in the seventh year
the land shall have a blessing of complete rest,

a sabbath of THE LORD:
you shall not sow your field or prune your vineyard.
You shall not reap the aftergrowth of your harvest
or gather the grapes of your untrimmed vines;
it shall be a year of complete rest for the land.
The land at rest shall yield your food.

Leviticus 25:2–6

---

[122] You shall count off 7 weeks of years—
7 x 7 years—
so that the period of 7 weeks of years
gives you a total of 49 years.
Then you shall sound the horn [*shofar*] loud;
in the seventh month, on the tenth day of the month—
the Day of Atonement—
you shall have the horn sounded throughout your land
and you shall hallow the fiftieth year.
You shall proclaim release throughout the land
for all its inhabitants....
you shall not sow,
neither shall you reap the aftergrowth
or harvest the untrimmed vines,
for it is a jubilee.
It shall be holy to you:
you may only eat growth direct from the field.

Leviticus 25:8–12

---

[123] At the heart of the sabbatical and jubilee legislation
seems to be the notion of inalienable ancestral subsistence land—
a small holding where each person could dwell
under one's own vine and fig tree, undisturbed (e.g., Micah 4:1-4).
This decentralized, agriculture-based model,
with the (extended) family unit assured a means of basic subsistence
in the form of land sufficient for its basic needs,
is the *liberty** to be proclaimed
throughout the land for all its inhabitants (Leviticus 25:10).
Applied to our own time and place,
it would result in a redistribution of wealth,

a decentralization of power,
and a redistribution of population toward more rural areas—
resulting in an immediate and direct relationship
to land and surroundings.

Rabbi Everett Gendler
The Third Jewish Catalog, p. 315 (adapted)

*or: release [NJV].

---

[124] It is a good custom for those who walk upright
to eat an abundance of fruit on this day
[Tu bi-Shvat, the New Year for Fruit/Nut Trees],
and to give expression to words of song and praise for them.

Peri Étz Hadar (Fruit of Goodly Trees)+
Land of Israel, 1700s

---

[125] It is a custom to give 91 coins as *tzedakah* (to sustain the needy)
on Tu bi-Shvat [the fifteenth day of the month *Shvat*]—
91 being the *gematria* (numerical equivalent)
for *ilan* (tree) and also for *mayim* (water),
which begins to enter the tree on this day [in the Land of Israel,
as the roots emerge from winter dormancy].
When Tu bi-Shvat falls on Monday night,
those whom God has blessed with riches
should give a portion of their money
to students of Torah and to the unfortunate
on the fourteenth of Shvat.
And even more so when Tu bi-Shvat falls on Saturday night—
because the Sabbath is over and they have nothing to buy fruit with,
and their children come to ask them for fruit,
but they are unable to buy anything
and they suffer more than in other years.
Happy is the one who has poor people and scholars of Torah
around the table on this night;
such a person will have God's blessing and will merit long life!

Rabbi Hayyim Palache+
Izmir, Turkey, 1788–1869
Moéd le-Khol Chai (1861)

[126] On Tu bi-Shvat
When spring comes,
An Angel descends, ledger in hand,
And enters each bud, each twig, each tree,
And all our garden flowers.
From town to town, from village to village
The angel makes a winged way,
Searching the valleys, inspecting the hills,
Flying over the desert
And returns to heaven.
And when the ledger will be full
Of trees and blossoms and shrubs,
When the desert is turned into a meadow
And all our land is a watered garden,
The Messiah will appear.

Shin Shalom (adapted)+
Poland/Vienna/Palestine/Israel, b. 1904

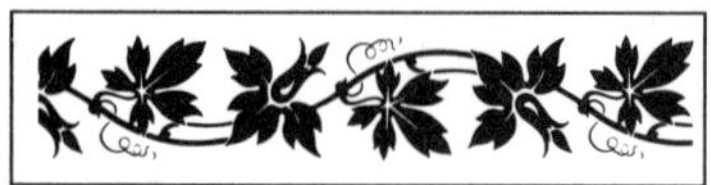

Spirituality

See also [7, 10, 27, 28, 29, 74, 76, 110, 111, 112, 160, 161, 162, 163, 181]

---

[127] Even if our
Mouths overflowed with song like the ocean's water
Tongues sang like surf
Lips praised sky-wide
Eyes shone sun and moon
Hands flying eagles
And *legs* swift gazelles—
We still could not thank You enough,
Our dear God and God of our ancestors,
For even one ten-thousandth of the wonders
Done for our ancestors and for us!

from *Nishmat Kol Chai*
[traditional Sabbath morning prayer;
part of a prayer about rain in Talmud of Babylonia, *Berakhot* 59b]
transl. Rabbi Levi Weiman–Kelman (adapted)

---

[128] Our Rabbis taught:[1]
"It's forbidden for you to enjoy (the use of) something in this world without first reciting a blessing;
anyone who enjoys something in this world without a blessing
has *misappropriated sacred property*"[2]....
Rabbi Levi posed a problem:
It is written: *The earth is* THE LORD*'s and all that it holds* (Psalms 24:1)
and it is also written: *The heavens belong to* THE LORD,
but the earth was given over to human beings (Psalms 115:16).
[Isn't there a contradiction here regarding the earth?]
No! The first verse applies to the situation that exists
before reciting a blessing;
the second verse—
after reciting a blessing!

Talmud of Babylonia, *Berakhot* 35a/b
c. 200–c. 600 CE

1. Cf. *Tosefta Berakhot* 4:1
2. *Me·i·lah*—a legal term that pertains to items donated to the Temple in Jerusalem.

---

[129] A heathen once asked Rabbi Joshua ben Korchah,
"Why did God choose a thornbush from which to speak to Moses?"
He answered, "Your question would have been the same
if it had been a carob tree or a sycamore;
but to dismiss you without any reply is not right,
so I will tell you why:
to teach you that no place is devoid of the divine Presence,
not even a thornbush."

Midrash Exodus Rabbah §2.5
Land of Israel, c. 1000 CE

---

[130] How can I fear mortals
When I have in me the Divine
Whose cubs scare away lions?
How can I fret about making ends meet
When inside me is Wisdom
From whose hills I can mine gems?
The sweets I crave are—within—my reach
Here's the brook that will quench my thirst.
How can I sit and mope
When it is I whom the Lute-Player
Serenades with a tune?
How can I make small-talk
When I could listen to my Guide make sense?
My lute with my voice are Its pen
My garden and my orchard, Its scroll.

Rabbi Judah ha-Levi
Spain, c.1075–1141 CE
transl. David E. Stein

[131] I see You in the starry field,
I see You in the harvest's yield,
In every breath, in every sound,
An echo of Your name is found.
The blade of grass, the simple flower,
Bear witness to Your matchless power,
In wonder-workings, or some bush aflame,
We look for God and fancy You concealed;
But in earth's common things You stand revealed
While grass and flowers and stars spell out Your name.

Rabbi Abraham Ibn Ezra+
Spain/Italy/Provence, 1089–1164 CE
transl. Rabbi Sidney Greenberg/Rabbi Jonathan D. Levine (adapted)

---

[132] In order to serve God,
one needs access
to the enjoyment of the beauties of nature,
such as the contemplation of flower-decorated meadows,
majestic mountains, flowing rivers, etc.
For all these are essential
to the spiritual development
of even the holiest of people.

Rabbi Abraham ben Maimonides+
Egypt, 1186–1237
quoted in *Ha-Mispik La-Avodat ha-Shem,* p. 165

---

[133] All that [we] see—
the heaven, the earth, and all that fills it—
all these things
are the external garments of God.

Rebbe Shneour Zalman+
Lyady, Belorussia, 1745–1813
Tanya §42 (1796)

---

[134] Know that all healing is of the earth—gifts of the trees—
especially potent during the month of *Iyyar* [May].

Rebbe Nahman of Bratslav+
Podolia, Ukraine, 1772–1810
Likkutei MoHaRaN §277

[135] Master of the Universe,
grant me the ability to be alone;
may it be my custom to go outdoors each day
among the trees and grass—among all growing things—
and there may I be alone, and enter into prayer,
to talk with the One to whom I belong.
May I express there everything in my heart,
and may all the foliage of the field—
all grasses, trees, and plants—
awake at my coming,
to send the powers of their life into the words of my prayer
so that my prayer and speech are made whole
through the life and spirit of all growing things,
which are made as one by their transcendent Source.
May I then pour out the words of my heart
before your Presence like water, O LORD,
and lift up my hands to You in worship,
on my behalf, and that of my children!

Rebbe Nahman of Bratslav+
Podolia, Ukraine, 1772–1810
transl. Rabbi Shamai Kanter (adapted)

---

[136] Once when Rav Abraham Isaac Kook*
was walking in the fields, lost deep in thought,
the young student with him
inadvertently plucked a leaf off a branch.
Rav Kook was visibly shaken by this act,
and turning to his companion he said gently,
"Believe me when I tell you
I never simply pluck a leaf or a blade of grass
or any living thing, unless I have to."
He explained further,
"Every part of the vegetable world is singing a song
and breathing forth a secret
of the divine mystery of the Creation."
For the first time the young student understood
what it means to show compassion to all creatures.

Wisdom of the Jewish Mystics, p. 80+

*Latvia/England/Palestine, 1865–1935

[137] Human beings have indeed become primarily tool-making animals,
and the world is now a gigantic tool box
for the satisfaction of their needs...
Nature as a tool box
is a world that does not point beyond itself.
It is when nature is sensed as mystery and grandeur
that it calls upon us to look beyond it.
The awareness of grandeur and the sublime
is all but gone from the modern mind.
The sense of the sublime—
the sign of inward greatness of the human soul
and something which is potentially given to all—
is now a rare gift.
Yet without it, the world becomes flat and the soul a vacuum.

Rabbi Abraham Joshua Heschel
Germany/USA, 1907–1972
God in Search of Man (1956), pp. 34, 36

[138] The best remedy
for those who are afraid, lonely, or unhappy
is to go outside,
somewhere where they can be quite alone
with the heavens, nature, and God.
Because only then does one feel that all is as it should be
and that God wishes to see people happy,
amidst the simple beauty of nature.
As long as this exists, and it certainly always will,
I know that then there will always be comfort for every sorrow....
And I firmly believe that nature brings solace in all troubles.

Diary of Anne Frank+
Anne Frank (1929–1945)

Sun

[139] God placed in the heavens a tent for the sun,
who is like a newlywed coming forth from the chamber,
like a champion, eager to run the course.
With a rising-place at one end of heaven,
and a circuit that reaches the other,
nothing escapes its heat.

Psalms 19:5–7

[140] The sun says:
The sun and moon stand still on high;
by the light of Your arrows do they go,
by the illumination of Your shining spear (Habakkuk 3:11).
And the sun says:
Arise, shine, for your light has dawned—
the Presence of THE LORD *will shine upon you!* (Isaiah 60:1)

Perek Shirah §2+
before 900 CE
[mystical collection of hymnic sayings
depicted as sung in praise of God
by all aspects of Creation]
transl. Rabbi J. David Bleich (adapted)

Torah

See also [46, 49]

---

[141] Happy is the one…whose delight is the teaching of THE LORD,
Who studies that teaching day and night.
Such a person is like a tree planted beside streams of water,
Which yields its fruit in season,
Whose foliage never fades,
And whatever it produces thrives.
Not so the wicked;
Rather, they are like chaff that wind blows away…

Psalms 1:1–4

---

[142] [Wisdom's] ways are pleasant ways,
And all her paths, peaceful.
She is a tree of life to those who grasp her,
And whoever holds on to her is happy.

Proverbs 3:17–18

---

[143] The Blessed Holy One said:
"See how beloved is Hebrew, the language of the Torah;
it is healing for the tongue!"
So the Bible says: *A healing tongue is a tree of life* (Proverbs 15:4);
and "tree of life" means Torah:
Wisdom is a tree of life to those who grasp her (Proverbs 3:18)….
In the future, God will bring forth the trees of the garden of Eden,
and they will heal the tongue:
All kinds of trees for food will grow up on both banks…
they will yield new fruit every month,
because the water for them flows from the Temple.
Their fruit will serve for food
and their leaves for healing (Ezekiel 47:12).

Midrash Deuteronomy Rabbah §1.1
Land of Israel, 800s CE

---

[144] One who tends a fig tree will enjoy its fruit,
And one who cares for a master will be honored.

Proverbs 27:18

---

[145] Rabbi Hiyya ben Abba said that Rabbi Yohanan said,
Why does the Bible say:
One who tends a fig tree will enjoy its fruit... (Proverbs 27:18)—
how are words of Torah like a fig tree?
Whenever you search a fig tree, you can find figs ready to eat.[1]
So also with words of Torah:
whenever you are engaged in studying them
you will find morsels of wisdom.[2]

Talmud of Babylonia, *Eruvin* 54a,b
c. 200–c. 600 CE

1. A tree's figs ripen at various times over a long season.
2. A pun in the Hebrew; *ta·am* means "wisdom" and also "taste."

---

[146] *On the day that Moses finished setting up the Tabernacle,*
he anointed and consecrated it... (Numbers 7:1).

✍ ✍ ✍

This bears on the text:
One who tends a fig tree will enjoy its fruit,
And one who cares for a master will be honored (Proverbs 27:18).
Why is Torah compared here to a fig tree?
Because most trees—olive, grape, date—
have their fruit picked at one time,
but the fig's fruit is picked gradually.
And so it is with the Torah:
you learn a little today and more tomorrow,
for you cannot learn it in one or two years....

Midrash Numbers Rabbah §12.9; 21.15 (repeated)
c. 1150–1200 CE

---

[147] *The Lord said to Joshua son of Nun, Moses' attendant,*
"...Prepare to cross...into the land I am giving to the Israelites....
As I was with Moses, so I will be with you..." (Joshua 1:1-5)

✍ ✍ ✍

Regarding this Scripture says:
One who tends a fig tree will enjoy its fruit,
And one who cares for a master will be honored (Proverbs 27:18).
Our Rabbis taught:
"If you see a fig in a dream, your Torah will be guarded for you,
as it is written, *One who tends a fig tree will enjoy its fruit.*"*
Another meaning:
Why is Torah compared to a fig?
Because every fruit has in it something inedible:
dates have pits, grapes have seeds, pomegranates have skin.
But every part of the fig is good to eat.
So too, words of Torah have nothing inedible, as it is written,
Take to heart all the words…of this Torah.
For it is not a worthless thing for you;
it is your very life (Deuteronomy 32:46-47).

Midrash Yalkut Shimoni ("Simeon's Collection"), Joshua §2
ed. Rabbi Simeon the Preacher, Frankfort, Germany, 1200s CE

*From Talmud of Babylonia, *Berakhot* 57a, which lists dream symbols—including fruit and animals—along with their meanings.

---

[148] Rabbi Tanhuma ben Abba opened his discourse:
You plucked up a vine from Egypt… (Psalms 80:9)
Why is Israel compared here to a grapevine?
When you want to improve its fruit,
you dig it up and replant it elsewhere and it improves.
So when the Holy One wanted to make Israel known in the world,
what did God do?
God uprooted them from Egypt
and brought them to the wilderness where they flourished.
They received the Torah and became known in the world.…

Midrash Exodus Rabbah §44.1
Land of Israel, c. 1000 CE

---

[149] …*If the pomegranates were in bloom…* (Song 6:11)

✍ ✍ ✍

These are the schoolchildren who sit and study Torah,
row by row, like pomegranate seeds.

Midrash Song of Songs Rabbah §1 on 6:11
Land of Israel, mid–500s CE

[150] *Like an apple among trees of the forest,*
So is my beloved among the youths.
I delight to sit in his shade,
And his fruit is sweet to my mouth (Song 2:3)

✍ ✍ ✍

Rabbis Huna and Aha said in the name of Rabbi Yose Ben Zimra,
"Why do people shun the apple tree when the sun beats down?
Because it provides no shade to sit under.
So did the peoples of the earth refuse to sit in the Holy One's shade
on the day the Torah was given.
Do you think that Israel was the same?
No, for it says, *I delight to sit in his shade—*
I delight in God and I *sit*; I and not the other nations."

Midrash Song of Songs Rabbah §1 on 2:3
Land of Israel, mid–500s CE

---

[151] Rabbi Simeon [bar Yohai][1] said:
One who walks along the road reviewing what has been taught,
and interrupts this study to say,
"How pleasant is that tree! How beautiful is that plowed field!"—
Torah regards such a person as if having committed a grave error.[2]

Mishnah *Pirké Avot* 3:7 (in prayer books: 3:9)
Land of Israel, c. 200 CE

1. In prayer books: Rabbi Jacob.
2. Literally: as if worthy of death. This phrase echoes the verse, *Recite these words when you walk along the road....so that you...may live long* (Deut. 11:19-21).

---

[152] Rabbi Simeon bar Yohai, Rabbi Eleazar, Rabbi Abba, and Rabbi Yose
were sitting one day beneath some trees
on the plain by the Sea of Ginnosar.*
Rabbi Simeon said
"The shade spread over us by these trees is so pleasant!
We must crown this place with words of Torah!"

Zohar (Book of Enlightenment) 2:127a
Rabbi Moses ben Shem Tov de Leon
Guadalajara, Spain, c. 1240–1305 CE
transl. Daniel Matt

*The narrow plain of Ginnosar on the northwestern shore
of the Sea of Galilee boasts fertile, volcanic soil.

Trees

See also [14, 16, 19–22, 24–26, 35, 37, 39, 42–44, 46, 47, 49, 50, 59, 60, 62, 63, 77, 83, 85, 88, 90, 102, 105, 107, 117, 118, 120, 126, 129, 134–136, 141–152, 174, 185–188, 190, 192, 194, 197]

---

[153] THE LORD God planted a garden in Eden, in the east,
and placed there the human being who had been formed.
And from the ground THE LORD God caused to grow
every tree that was pleasing to the sight and good for food,
with the tree of life in the middle of the garden,
and the tree of knowledge of good and bad.

Genesis 2:8–9

---

[154] When you enter the land and plant any tree for food,
you shall regard its fruit as its foreskin.
Three years it shall be uncircumcised for you, not to be eaten.
In the fourth year all its fruit shall be set aside
for jubilation before THE LORD;
and only in the fifth year may you use its fruit—
that its yield to you may be increased:
I THE LORD am your God.*

Leviticus 19:23–25
transl. Rabbi Howard Eilberg–Schwartz, based on NJV.

*This ensures the development of the root systems and the healthy growth of the young sapling's trunk and branches, especially if the grower takes care to remove the flowers [Nogah Hareuveni]. As a rule, the types of fruit trees growing in the Land of Israel do not bear fruit until the fourth year and beyond [Eilberg-Schwartz].

---

[155] Rabbi Judah ben Simon began his discourse with the text:
Follow[1] *none but THE LORD your God...!* (Deuteronomy 13:5)
But can a person of flesh and blood follow the Blessed Holy One—
the One of whom it is written:
Your path was through the mighty waters;
Your tracks could not be seen (Psalms 77:20)?
Yet you say, *Follow none but THE LORD your God...*

and hold fast to no one else! (Deuteronomy 13:5)
But can a person of flesh and blood go up to heaven
to hold fast to the divine Presence—
the One of whom it is written: *a consuming fire* (Deuteronomy 4:24),
whose *throne is tongues of flame* (Daniel 7:9)
and before whom *a river of fire streams forth* (Daniel 7:10)?
Yet you say, *hold fast to no one else!*
In truth, the Blessed Holy One,
from the very start of the creation of the world,
was occupied before all else with *planting*:
And first of all[2] *THE LORD God planted a garden in Eden* (Genesis 2:8).
Therefore, when you are in the Land of Israel,
occupy yourselves first and foremost with planting.
Hence it is written,
When you come into the land, you shall plant... (Leviticus 19:23).

Midrash Leviticus Rabbah §25.3
Land of Israel, c. 450 CE

1. Literally: walk after.
2. The Hebrew *mi-ke·dem,* usually rendered "in the east," can also mean "first of all."

---

[156] *When you enter the Land of Israel*
you shall plant[1] *all kinds of trees for food...* (Leviticus 19:23)

✍ ✍ ✍

It is said: *Who put wisdom in the hidden parts?*
Who gave understanding to the rooster? (Job 38:36)....
The hen, when its young are tiny,
gathers them together and places them beneath its wings,
warming them and grubbing for them.
But when they are grown up, if one of them wants to get near her,
she pecks it on the head and says to it, "Go grub your own dunghill!"
So during the forty years that Israel were in the wilderness:
the manna fell, the well came up for them, the quail were at hand,
the cloud of glory encircled them, and the pillar of cloud led the way.
When Israel were about to enter the Land of Israel,
Moses said to them:
"Let every one of you take a shovel and go out and plant trees!"[2]

Midrash Leviticus Rabbah §25.5
Land of Israel, c. 450 CE

1. Or: and you plant.
2. What follows this passage is a comic tale about a Jew who plants a fig tree.

---

[157] *When you enter the Land of Israel*
you shall plant all kinds of trees for food...* (Leviticus 19:23).

The Holy One said to Israel:
"Even if you find the land full of all good things,
you should not say, 'We will sit and not plant';
rather, be diligent in planting!
Just as you came and found trees planted by others,
you must plant for your children;
a person must not say, 'I am old, how many years will I live? Why should I get up and exert myself for others?
I'm going to die tomorrow.'
You must not excuse yourself from planting.
As you found trees, plant more, even if you are old."

Midrash Tanhuma, Kedoshim+
Land of Israel, after 800 CE

*or: and you plant.

---

[158] "Like a lily among thorns,
So is my darling among the maidens."
"Like an apple tree among trees of the forest,
So is my beloved among the youths;
I delight to sit in his shade,
And his fruit is sweet to my mouth."

Song of Songs 2:2–3

---

[159] For now the winter is past,
The rains are over and gone.
The blossoms have appeared in the land,
The time of pruning* has come;
The song of the turtledove
Is heard in our land.
The green figs form on the fig tree,
The vines in blossom give off fragrance.
Arise, my darling;
My fair one, come away!

Song of Songs 2:11–13

*or: singing.

[160] Your limbs are an orchard of pomegranates
And of all luscious fruits,
Of henna and of nard—nard and saffron,
Fragrant reed and cinnamon,
With all aromatic woods, myrrh and aloes—
All the choice perfumes.

Song of Songs 4:13

[161] Your brow behind your veil
[Gleams] like a pomegranate split open.

Song of Songs 6:7

[162] I went down to the nut grove
To see the budding of the vale;
To see if the vines had blossomed,
If the pomegranates were in bloom.

Song of Songs 6:11

[163] Your stately form is like the palm,
Your breasts are like clusters.
I say: Let me climb the palm,
Let me take hold of its branches;
Let your breasts be like clusters of grapes,
Your breath like the fragrance of apples,
And your mouth like choicest wine!

Song of Songs 7:8–10

[164] The roots of the fig tree are soft
but they break through the hard stone.

Talmud of the Land of Israel, *Ta'anit* 1:3
c. 200–c. 400 CE

[165] Rabbi Yohanan ben Zakkai received Torah from Hillel and Shammai....

He used to say:
If you have a sapling in your hand,
and someone should say to you that the Messiah has come,
stay and complete the transplanting,
and then go welcome the Messiah.

Avot de-Rabbi Natan B §31
c. 200–700 CE

[166] ...This is the general rule:
for any main dish accompanied by a side dish,
you say a blessing only over the main dish.

Mishnah *Berakhot* 6:7
Land of Israel, c. 200 CE

....Said Rabbi Aha, son of Rabbi Avira said Rabbi Ashi,
"That rule is taught with regard to those who eat fruit from Ginnosar."[1]
....Rabbi Abbahu ate them until a fly would slip off his forehead.[2]
Rabbi Ammi and Rabbi Assi kept eating them until their hair fell out.
Rabbi Simeon ben Lakish kept eating them
to the point that he became confused.
Rabbi Yohanan reported that to the house of the patriarch,
and Rabbi Judah the Patriarch sent a band of officials after him
to bring him home.

Talmud of Babylonia, *Berakhot* 44a
c. 200–c. 600 CE

1. The narrow plain of Ginnosar on the northwestern shore of the Sea of Galilee boasts fertile, volcanic soil.

2. Apparently, the fruit made his skin that smooth.

---

[167] Rabbi Yohanan said:
What illustrates the verse:
...*one who hardens the heart falls into misfortune* (Proverbs 28:14)?
....That through the shaft of a litter, Bétar[1] was destroyed:
It was a custom in Bétar when a boy was born to plant a cedar tree,
and when a girl was born, a pine[2] tree;
when two people married, a wedding canopy was made of the branches.
One day the emperor's daughter was passing nearby
when a shaft of her litter broke;
so they chopped branches off a cedar tree and brought them to her.
The Jews then fell upon them and beat them up.
It was reported to the emperor that the Jews were rebelling,
and he marched against them.

Talmud of Babylonia, *Gittin* 57a
c. 200–c. 600 CE

1. A fortified town southwest of Jerusalem, destroyed by three Roman legions in 135 CE in response to a revolt.

2. Others: cypress.

[168] Said Rabbi Yohanan:
All his life, the righteous Honi the Circle-maker was troubled by this verse:
When THE LORD restored the fortunes of Zion—
we were like dreamers—[1]... (Psalms 126:1)
He thought, "Can someone really dream for 70 years?!"[2]
Once Honi the Circle-maker was walking on the road
and saw a man planting a carob tree.
Honi said: "You know a carob tree takes 70 years to bear fruit;[3]
are you so sure that you will live 70 years so as to eat from it?"
"I found this world provided with carob trees," the man replied,
"and as my forebears planted them for me,
so will I plant for my offspring."
Honi then sat down to eat and was overcome with sleep.
As he slept, a small cave formed around him, so that he was hidden.
And thus he slept for 70 years.
When he awoke,
he saw a man gathering carobs from that same tree, and eating them.
"Do you know who planted this carob tree?" Honi asked.
"My grandfather," the man replied.
"I must have been like a dreamer for 70 years!" Honi exclaimed....

Talmud of Babylonia, *Ta'anit* 23a
c. 200–c. 600 CE
transl. based on H. Malter

1. NJV: we see it as in a dream [meaning of Hebrew uncertain]

2. understanding the verse to refer to the Babylonian exile; about 70 years elapsed between the destruction of the First Temple in Jerusalem (c. 586 BCE) and the dedication of the Second Temple (515 BCE) [cf. Jer. 29:10].

3. Female carobs begin to bear fruit at a later age than other fruit trees. And the male carob when very old begins to produce female flowers and fruit. [Judah Feliks]

---

[169] On barren hills we plant the slip
Who shall not taste the tree.
The lengthening root, the ripening fruit
We may not hope to see.
But oh, the joy of planting trees
And oh, the keen delight
When unafraid beneath their shade
We rest in dreams at night.

Jessie E. Sampter
USA/Palestine, 1883–1938

Unity of All Things

See also [5, 30, 34, 52, 76, 114, 115, 135, 140]

---

[170] *Heaven and earth were finished—*
all their array[1] (Genesis 2:1).

✍ ✍ ✍

Rabbi Simon said: Every single herb has a constellation in the sky
that hits it and says to it, "Grow!"[2]
as it is written: *Do you know the laws of heaven*
Or impose its authority [mish·ta·ro][3] *on earth?* (Job 38:33)
Can you tie cords [ma·a·da·not] *of Pleiades*
Or undo the reins [mosh·khot] *of Orion?* (Job 38:31)
Rabbi Hanina ben Papa and Rabbi Simon said:
The Pleiades invigorates *[me·a·de·net]* the produce [in winter];
Orion stretches *[mo·shékh]* [it] from knot to knot [in summer].
Can you lead out Mazzarot in its season...? (Job 38:32)
Rabbi Tanhum ben Rabbi Hiyya and Rabbi Simon said:
That's the constellation that ripens *[me·maz·zér]* produce.

Midrash Genesis Rabbah §10.6
Land of Israel, c. 400 CE

1. The Hebrew *tza·va* (array, hosts) can connote rigorous—even military—service.
2. Underlings sometimes encounter violence at the hands of their superiors.
3. Rabbi Simon connects *mishtaro* with *shotér* (overseer) and *shtar* (Aramaic: to hit).

---

[171] Every blade of grass below
has a guardian official* above.

Zohar (Book of Enlightenment) §1:34a;
2:30b; 2:171b; 3:86a; errata 1:251 (c. 1286 CE)
Rabbi Moses ben Shem Tov de Leon
Guadalajara, Spain, c. 1240–1305 CE

*variously: powerful officer, celestial chieftain, star and constellation.

[172] Rabbi Yose once told this story:
"It happened when I was out walking with my son Rabbi Hiyya,
that we came upon a man collecting medicinal herbs....
He said, 'If people but knew the wisdom
of all that the Blessed Holy One has planted in the earth,
and the power of all that is to be found in the world,
they would proclaim the power of their LORD...!
But the Holy One has purposely hidden this wisdom from humans....'"
Rabbi Simeon [bar Yohai] later said:
"It is indeed as he said!...
There is no herbage in which God's wisdom is not greatly manifested
and which cannot exert great influence in heaven....
For people to purify themselves from ritual contamination,
the hyssop is used as a means of purification....
The power above that is represented by that herb...
is roused to wipe out the spirit of contamination..."

Zohar (Book of Enlightenment), §2:80a/b (c. 1286)
Rabbi Moses ben Shem Tov de Leon
Guadalajara, Spain, c. 1240–1305

[173] *If you lend money to My people—*
to the poor one who is in your power—
do not act toward such a person as a creditor:
exact no interest... (Exodus 22:24).

✍ ✍ ✍

It is written: *All goes well with one who lends generously,*
who conducts affairs with equity (Psalms 112:5).
Observe how all God's creations borrow from one another:
day borrows from night, and night from day;[1]
but they then do not sue one another as mortals do—
Day to day speaks out/Night to night relates what is known...
Not a sound is heard (Psalms 19:3).
The moon borrows[2] from the stars, and the stars from the moon....
The heavens borrow from the earth, and earth from the heavens—
THE LORD will open for you that bounteous store—the heavens—
to provide rain for your land... (Deuteronomy 28:12)....
Those who exact usury in effect say to God:
"Why don't you insist on payment from us—
payment for the earth that You water;
for the flowers You make grow;
for the lights You make shine;
for the soul You have breathed into us;
for the body you watch over?"
God says to them: "See how much I have lent,
yet *I* have not taken interest...!"

Midrash Exodus Rabbah §31.15
Land of Israel, c. 1000 CE

1. As the seasons change, so does the length of day/night.
2. in terms of relative brightness, as the moon waxes and wanes.

---

[174] Said Dov Baer,* the Preacher of Mezhirech [in the Ukraine]:
Your kind deeds
are used by God
as seed for the planting of trees in the garden of Eden;
thus, each of you creates your own Paradise.

Esser Orot (Ten Lights)+

*d.1772.

Waste Disposal

---

[175] There shall be an area for you outside the military camp,
where you may relieve yourself.
With your gear you shall have a spike,
and when you have squatted
you shall dig a hole with it and cover up your excrement.
Since THE LORD your God moves about in your camp
to protect you and to deliver your enemies to you,
let your camp be holy;
let God not find anything unseemly among you
and turn away from you.

Deuteronomy 23:13–15

---

[176] One who had put away thorns or broken glass[1]
[in the public domain]...
and others are injured by them
is liable for their injury....

Mishnah *Baba Kamma* 3:2
Land of Israel, c. 200 CE

✍ ✍ ✍

....Our rabbis taught:
"The pious ones of old
used to hide their thorns and broken glass in the midst of their fields
at a depth of three handbreadths below the surface
so that even the plow could not be hindered by them."
Rabbi Sheshet used to throw them into the fire.
Raba threw them into the Tigris River.[2]
Rab Judah said: "One who wishes to be truly pious
must be sure to attend to matters regarding liability."
But Raba said: "...matters regarding ethics."
Others said: "...matters regarding the reciting of blessings."

Talmud of Babylonia, *Baba Kamma* 30a
c. 200–c. 600 CE

1. That is, hazardous waste that one has made an effort to dispose of.
2. Cf. Maimonides' *Mishneh Torah, Laws of Monetary Damages* §13.22.

[177] It once happened that a farmer
was removing stones from a field
and putting them onto a public thoroughfare.
There was a certain pious person who challenged the farmer:
"Why are you taking stones from what is not yours
and putting them onto what belongs to you?"
The farmer just laughed.
Some time afterward, that farmer fell into need and sold the field.
Walking along in that very place,
the farmer stumbled on the rocks, and said,
"It was not for nothing that that pious one said to me,
'Look, you are removing stones from what is not yours
and putting them onto what belongs to you!'"

Tosefta Baba Kamma 10:2
Land of Israel, c. 400 CE;
cf. Talmud of Babylonia, *Baba Kamma* 50b

---

[178] The tannery [—which produces foul odors—]
is located at least 50 cubits [75 feet] from the city limit.
A tannery can only be operated on the east side
[downwind] of the city.

Mishnah *Baba Batra* 2:9
Land of Israel, c. 200 CE

---

[179] The quality of urban air
compared to the air in the deserts and forests
is like thick and turbulent water compared to pure and light water....
In the cities with their tall buildings and narrow roads,
the pollution that comes from their residents, their waste,
...makes their entire air reeking... and thick,...
although no one is aware of it....
Because we grow up in cities and become used to them,
we can at least choose a city with an open horizon...
And if you...cannot move out of the city,
try at least to...let the house be tall and the court wide enough
to permit the northern wind and the sun to come through,
because the sun thins out the pollution of the air...

Rabbi Moses Maimonides+
Fostat, Egypt, 1135–1204 CE
"The Preservation of Youth"

Water

See also [22, 34, 38, 43, 46, 48, 51, 54, 59, 61, 64, 65, 84, 97, 127, 132, 141]

---

[180] All streams flow into the sea,
Yet the sea is never full.
To the place from which the water flows,
there it returns.

Ecclesiastes 1:7

Wise Use

[*See also* 3, 6, 7, 9, 10, 11, 17, 20, 21, 92, 94, 128, 168, 177, 178]

---

[181] God blessed them [the first human beings] and God said to them,
"Be fertile and increase,
fill the earth and master it;
and rule the fish of the sea,
the birds of the sky,
and all the living things that creep on earth!"

Genesis 1:28

---

[182] *God said, "I will make humankind in My image, after My likeness.*
They shall rule [ve-yir·du]... *the whole earth"....*
God blessed them and God said to them,
"Be fertile and increase, fill the earth and master it;
and rule [u-re·du]... *all living things... "* (Genesis 1:28).

✍ ✍ ✍

Rabbi Hanina said:
"If humankind merits it, God says *u-re·du* [rule!];
while if humankind does not merit it,
God says *yé·ra·du* [let them (the animals) rule]."*

Midrash Genesis Rabbah §8.12
Land of Israel, c. 400 CE

*Or: let them [human beings] descend [from their position of mastery].

---

[183] When you besiege a city for a long time—
making war against it in order to take it—
you shall not destroy its trees
by wielding an axe against them.
You may eat from them,
but you must not cut them down!
Are trees of the field human beings
to withdraw before you into the besieged city?*

Only trees that you know are not food-bearing
you may destroy and cut down,
in order to build siege-works
against the city that makes war with you,
until it falls.

Deuteronomy 20:19–20

*Or: for the trees of the field equal human lives; they are not to be besieged by you.

---

[184] If, along the road, you chance upon a bird's nest
in any tree or on the ground—
with fledglings or eggs
and the mother sitting over the fledglings or on the eggs—
do not take the mother together with her young.
Let the mother go!
Take only the young,
in order that you may fare well and have a long life.

Deuteronomy 22:6–7

---

[185] ...*the trees of the field equal human lives...* (Deuteronomy 20:19)

✍ ✍ ✍

This shows that human livelihood depends upon trees...

Midrash Sifré to Deuteronomy §203 *(Shofetim)*
Land of Israel, c. 400 CE

---

[186] ...*you shall not destroy its trees*
by wielding an axe against them (Deuteronomy 20:19).

✍ ✍ ✍

You might think that this refers only to destruction by means of iron.
How do we infer that it also means that you must not shift a water conduit from them?*
Because it is stated [categorically]
you shall not destroy its trees—
that is, by any means.

Midrash Sifré to Deuteronomy §203 *(Shofetim)*
Land of Israel, c. 400 CE

*Cf. 2 Chronicles 32:2-4; when Assyrian armies invaded the kingdom of Judah, King Hezekiah stopped up sources of water so that the enemy could not use them.

[187] *"Only trees that you know*[1] (this means a food tree [past its prime]) *are not food-bearing* (this means a barren[2] tree) *you may destroy and cut down…* (Deuteronomy 20:19)."

"But if in the end we include both kinds of trees [as eligible to be cut down], why did the Torah explicitly say, *not food-bearing*?"

"When given a choice, [cut down] a barren tree instead of a food tree."

"And when does this rule apply? You might infer that [the Torah meant for us *always* to cut down a barren tree first], even if [when left standing] it would have a higher market value [than the fruit tree's future yield]; but the Torah text says [to cut the barren tree first] *only* [when the market value for the two types of trees is *equal.* (In general, relative market values should be used to decide which tree to cut down first.)]"

Midrash Sifré to Deuteronomy §204 *(Shofetim)*
Land of Israel, c. 400 CE;
also Talmud of Babylonia, *Baba Kamma* 91b–92a
transl. David E. Stein

1. The Hebrew connotes "have experience with."
2. any species that does not produce edible fruit or nuts.

[188] Rav said, "A date palm that yields a *kav*[1] of fruit—it is forbidden to chop it down. [If it yields less, you may chop it down. The deciding factor is the yield.]"

But [Mishnah *Shevi'it* 4:10 seems to contradict that claim:] "How much must an olive tree [yield] that it not be chopped down? A quarter [of a *kav].*" [So which volume of fruit is the correct minimal yield?]

[Resolution:] Olives are different in that they are more valuable. [A quarter-*kav* of olives is thus worth the same as a *kav* of dates. What counts is not volume but rather market value.]

Rabbi Hanina said, "My son Shivhat passed away for the sole reason that he cut down a fig tree before its time."[2]

Ravina said, "If [his tree] would have been worth more [when chopped down, as compared to the value of its fruit yield, then cutting it down] would have been permitted. [The proper decision procedure is to assess the net benefit based on market values.]"

Talmud of Babylonia, *Baba Kamma* 91b
c. 200–c. 600 CE
transl. David E. Stein

1. A measure of volume, like a bushel.
2. Illustrates literally …*the trees of the field equal human lives…* (Deut. 20:19)

[189] Whenever Rav Hisda had to walk among thorns and thistles,
he used to lift up his garment, saying,
"If my body is scratched, it will heal itself;
but if my garment is torn, it will not heal itself."

Talmud of Babylonia, *Baba Kamma* 91b
c. 200–c. 600 CE
cf. *Ta'anit* 23a

[190] Our Rabbis have taught:
"One who buys a tree from a friend for felling
shall leave the height of a handbreadth from the ground,
and then cut it."*

Talmud of Babylonia, *Baba Batra* 80b
c. 200–c. 600 CE

*so that a stump remains from which a new tree can grow.

[191] Our Rabbis taught:[1]
"A lump of salt may be placed in a lamp [before the Sabbath]
in order that it burns brightly [on the Sabbath];[2]
likewise, mud and clay may be placed under a lamp
so that it burns slowly."[3]
Rabbi Zutra said:
One who covers an oil lamp
or uncovers a naphtha lamp
violates *bal tashchit (You must not destroy…!)*.[4]

Talmud of Babylonia, *Shabbat* 67b
c. 200–c. 600 CE

1. Cf. *Tosefta Shabbat* 2:7.
2. Salt clarifies the oil.
3. Their mass absorbs heat, keeping the oil cooler and hence thicker.
4. These acts reduce the efficiency of the lamp.

---

[192] *Make the planks for the Tabernacle of acacia wood...* (Exodus 26:15).

✍ ✍ ✍

Why of acacia wood?
God set an example for all time,
that when we are about to build a house from a food tree,
we should be reminded:
If when God commanded the Sanctuary to be erected,
the instructions were to use only barren* trees—
even though all things belong to God—
how much more should this be the case with wood for our own house!

Midrash Exodus Rabbah §35.2
Land of Israel, c. 1000 CE

*any species that does not produce edible fruit or nuts.

---

[193] It is forbidden to cut down food trees* outside a [besieged] city, nor may a water channel be deflected from them so that they wither, as it is said: *You must not destroy its trees!* (Deuteronomy 20:19). Whoever cuts down a food tree is flogged [39 times].

And not only during a siege: whenever a food tree is cut down with destructive intent, flogging is incurred. But it may be cut down when:

- it damages other trees; or
- it damages a field belonging to someone else; or
- its value for other purposes is greater [than that of its food yield].

The Torah forbids only *wanton* destruction.

Rabbi Moses Maimonides
Fostat, Egypt, 1135–1204 CE
Mishneh Torah, Book of Judges, Laws of Kings and Wars §6.8
[first comprehensive, systematic rabbinic legal code
with commentary, c. 1178 CE]

*i.e., trees that bear fruit or nuts.

---

[194] One is permitted to cut down a barren* tree
even if one does not need it.
So too, an old food tree that produces an amount too small to bother with
may be cut down....

Rabbi Moses Maimonides
Fostat, Egypt, 1135–1204 CE
Mishneh Torah, Book of Judges, Laws of Kings and Wars §6.9

*any species that does not bear edible fruit or nuts.

[195] Not only one who cuts down food trees, but also one who smashes household goods, tears clothes, demolishes a building, stops up a spring, or destroys food on purpose violates the command: *You must not destroy...!* (Deuteronomy 20:19). Such a person is administered a disciplinary beating.*

Rabbi Moses Maimonides
Fostat, Egypt, 1135–1204
Mishneh Torah, Book of Judges, Laws of Kings and Wars §6.10

*Severity of punishment is at the discretion of the judge, for these crimes are forbidden by the Torah only indirectly.

[196] This biblical commandment [*bal tash·chit (You must not destroy...!)*]
prohibits the spoiling of any object
from which humankind may benefit.

Rebbe Shneour Zalman
Lyady, Belorussia, 1745–1813
Shulchan Arukh ha-Rav, Choshen Mishpat:
Hilkhot Shemirat Guf va-Nefesh §14

[197] If a person kills a tree before its time,
it is like having murdered a soul.*

Rebbe Nahman of Bratslav+
Podolia, Ukraine, 1772–1810

*Cf. [105] in this booklet.

[198] This prohibition
of purposeless destruction of food trees around a besieged city
is only to be taken as an example of general wastefulness.
Under the concept of *bal tash·chit (You must not destroy...!)*,
the purposeless destruction of anything at all is taken to be forbidden,
so that our text becomes
the most comprehensive warning to human beings
not to misuse the position that God has given them

as masters of the world and its matter
to capricious, passionate, or merely thoughtless wasteful destruction
of anything on earth.
Only for *wise use* has God laid the world at our feet
when God said to humankind,
...fill the earth and master it; and rule...! (Genesis 1:28)

Rabbi Samson Raphael Hirsch
Germany, 1808–1888
The Pentateuch: Translated and Explained [German] (1878)
comment on Deuteronomy 20:20
transl. Isaac Levy (adapted)
Cf. *Horeb: Essays on Israel's "Duties" in the Diaspora* §56 (1837)

---

[199] A season is set for everything,
  a time for every experience under heaven:
A time for being born
  and a time for dying,
A time for planting
  and a time for uprooting the planted;
A time for slaying
  and a time for healing,
A time for tearing down
  and a time for building up.

Ecclesiastes 3:1–3

---

[200] *Consider God's doing!*
Who can straighten what has been twisted? (Ecclesiastes 7:13)

✍ ✍ ✍

When God created the first human beings,
God led them around the garden of Eden and said:
"Look at my works!
See how beautiful they are—how excellent!
For your sake I created them all.
See to it that you do not spoil and destroy My world;
for if you do, there will be no one else to repair it."

Midrash Ecclesiastes Rabbah §1 on 7:13
c. 800 CE

Index of Sources

Passages that are cited by another source or in the footnotes are listed here in *italics*.

Hebrew Bible

Early Rabbinic Texts

Later Rabbinic Sources

Other Sources

Colophon

A Garden of Choice Fruit was designed using Quark XPress® on a Macintosh® computer. The typefaces are Zapf Dingbats and Adobe System Incorporated's ITC Clearface® Family: Regular, Regular Italic, Bold, Bold Italic, Heavy, Heavy Italic, and Black. The cover is printed on 80# Cameo Ivory Recycled Cover; the text pages are 55# PC Book Antique Recycled Text. The flower design for the cover was originally published in *The Art of William Morris* by Aymer Vallance, as published by George Bell & Sons, London, 1897.